MW01260197

AWAKE

Achieve Your Goals and Change Your Life

TO YOUR

with the 5 AM Advantage

WHY

BRYCE CHAPMAN

RIVER GROVE
BOOKS

Published by River Grove Books
Austin, TX
www.rivergrovebooks.com

Distributed by River Grove Books

Design and composition by Greenleaf Book Group
Cover design by Greenleaf Book Group and John van der Woude

Publisher's Cataloging-in-Publication data is available.

Paperback ISBN: 978-1-63299-778-4

eBook ISBN: 978-1-63299-779-1

Hardcover ISBN: 978-1-63299-789-0

First Edition

To my why—
my incredible wife, Fiona, and beautiful children,
Jess, Ollie, Oscar, and Brooke

CONTENTS

CHARGING BULLS

One day in 2008, I reached into the back of the truck to grab the rear leg of a piglet. It immediately went into panic mode and exploded in alarm, struggling and fighting against my efforts as if its life depended on its escape. The deafening squeal rang in my ears as I carried it down the driveway, through the side gate, and into the school's playground.

I had carried hundreds of piglets over nearly two decades of teaching children about life on the farm, but this day was different. It was my birthday. And instead of spending the day relaxing at home, I was at work for my company Kindifarm, Australia's largest mobile animal farm. I had started it from scratch in 1992, with two hundred flyers and a lot of blood, sweat, and tears.

As I—a forty-two-year-old man with a university degree—struggled with that squealing piglet in front of a bunch of snot-nosed kids, I looked incredulously at what I was doing. I felt regret, overwhelm, and panic—sick in the guts.

How did I get here? I thought. *There must be something better than this.*

I recognized a feeling I had been living with for a while but didn't want to confront: I wasn't in control of my life. I wasn't doing what I really wanted to do, whatever that was. I had reached a breaking point, and I knew something had to change.

Even though I didn't realize it in the moment, I know now that that day was a long time coming. The path to my breaking point had started years earlier when my fifth-grade class was interrupted by the news that my father was killed when his light plane crashed. When my family suffered, and I was forced to become the man of the house without the guidance of my hero. When we packed up everything and moved from the country to the city and from a small school to a large one. When weekend binge drinking became the norm. When I began to resent the hand life had dealt me.

Still, I put my head down and worked hard over the next couple of decades, becoming what many call successful. I had a growing business, new cars, a seaside house, and a country farm. Behind all that, however, were long and hard days at work, staff issues, large mortgages, piles of bills to be paid, a failed marriage, responsibility, commitment, and stress. But I kept my nose to the grindstone, day after day, month after month, and year after year. After all, that was what success looked like. Everyone around me seemed happy with my achievements and ability to push through adversity toward, well, who knows where.

That day at the school with the piglet, after those years of busyness and stress, I finally said, "Enough is enough. No more. I need to change this now!" I made a split-second decision: I would set tomorrow's alarm for 5 AM. But this time, I would kick-start a new goal, a new habit, a new life. I saw that intention as a simple transformative act, an unavoidable reminder that it was time to rise and live a better life.

The decision to wake up at 5 AM wasn't random. I remembered that I had used this tactic before to achieve another goal: finishing the Hay, Hell to Booligal Endurance Ride. This thing was an epic horseback ride that started in the town of Hay, followed the desolate Cobb Highway across the Hell of the Hay Plains (one of the flattest sections of land in the world), and finished fifty miles north in the small, isolated outpost town of Booligal.

As a twenty-two-year-old jackaroo working on an outback sheep and cattle station, I was unwinding in the local pub one day, enjoying a well-earned beer, when I noticed a poster on the wall for this annual horse event. *All right*, I thought, guzzling down more beer. *Now that's an adventure!*

Suddenly, heart racing, I was aware of what I was about to do. In that moment, I decided to prove myself to be a horseman like my father and challenged myself to enter the legendary race. For most competitors, simply completing the ride was the objective. But I was committed to more—I was committed to a dream, a holy mission to uphold my birthright in the saddle. And I didn't want to fail.

Knowing I needed to prepare well, I set myself the challenge of waking at 5 AM each day to ride my horse Blue Boy, named after my childhood pony. We'd go out to the station's boundary fence and back. The station spread over 56,000 acres, so the back fence was well out of sight, giving plenty of saddle time for both horse and rider. The sun rose over the vast open space with magnificent shades of red and orange and filled me with exhilaration. As we trotted toward the horizon, the crispness of the morning air surged through my lungs, and the rhythm in the saddle connected me with the pounding hoofs of my steed.

We were back at the homestead before breakfast, and I would experience a powerful sense of achievement—of synergy—knowing that Blue Boy and I were becoming one and that I was becoming a competent horse rider. I was betting everything on myself and stepping up to meet the challenge. All before my regular day began.

Race day came. Not surprisingly, I was fearful, but the months of disciplined training paid off. Blue Boy and I rode across the outback in the blistering heat, the temperature rising to over 113°F (45°C) on the unshaded road. My shirt was drenched with sweat and sticking to my chest. My arms burned in the sun. We pushed on throughout the day, following the straight line of the telephone poles as they disappeared ahead of us into the hypnotizing mirage of heat waves. Hour after hour passed as I dug deep, my grit and determination muzzling the demons in my mind. *You're going to make it, Bryce*, I grunted. *Just step up. Keep stepping up!*

We rode. And rode. Finally, I could make out dots in the distance. Relief washed over me. The dots slowly grew into the town of Booligal, and the usually deserted streets welcomed us from Hell with the comforting sounds of cheering and encouragement.

Crossing the finish line, I could barely dismount. After nine hours and thirteen minutes of riding, my fatigued body cramped and exhaustion took hold—but we had done it! I'd pushed beyond my perceived capability and out of my comfort zone. That poster on the pub wall and that moment of purpose and clarity had put me on a course of action, and I'd succeeded.

"Yes!" I screamed at the top of my lungs. "Yes! Yes! We did it!" I told Blue Boy, tears in my eyes. For months, I'd dedicated my life, my sweat, my resolve, my heart, and my entire existence to this one moment. I had become obsessed.

The other reason for setting my alarm for 5 AM also wasn't random. I had been aspiring to wake up earlier for a few years, anyway. However, it had been intermittent and only a morning or two each week at best—often, not at all. It was not a habit. It was not an obsession. Up until that day with the piglet, I hadn't had a burning desire like when I was twenty-two, deciding to ride my horse across the outback. But that day, I had a breakthrough. I knew that I wanted, more than anything in the world, to live a better life. Being fully committed to waking up at 5 AM had worked before, so maybe, I thought, it would work again.

And it did.

A decade after that decision to fully commit myself to waking up early, my life had radically changed for the better. I woke up at 5 AM most mornings to exercise. I was healthier and happier. I had restructured my business focus to run it with a fraction of effort while dramatically increasing my income. My wife and children enjoyed a greatly improved lifestyle. I spent more time with friends and family. I had time to map out my life and make decisions. I had time to follow my dreams. Life was outstanding.

I also decided to research and write about the habit of early rising. I am passionate about the practice, but over the years, I have experienced the good, the bad, and the ugly in those waking moments. Waking at 5 AM is unquestionably a challenge. A challenge, by definition, is not easy, but my life then was proof that the payoff is exponentially greater than the effort of getting out of bed. I also realized it wasn't enough to simply wake up at 5 AM. To be successful—that is, to take massive action to achieve my goals—I had to learn to be intentional about the process. I started writing down the strategies I used to leverage my early waking time and propel myself forward. It had worked for me, and I wanted to share my experience with others.

My writings turned out to be the beginnings of a book—this book—a manual for others who, like me, find themselves at a breaking point. It's for those who have ignored a dream for too long or who have not let an idea grow. For those who feel lost and are missing their *why*. For those who need a strategy to take back control of their lives.

And then, in 2016, I was charged by a bull.

And it derailed my book project, my health, and my life.

And it put the strategy I developed—what I call the 5 AM Advantage—to the ultimate test.

—

My family's farm is a cattle-breeding operation, 125 miles north of Sydney. One blazing hot Saturday, we were having a great weekend, tending the horses, feeding the cattle, and sweating through the chores that keep us busy.

Earlier that day, I'd noticed a bull among our herd. He was busy sniffing the in-season females in preparation to do what bulls do best. He'd boldly forced himself through the boundary fence from the neighbor, and I needed to move the bull quickly before he impregnated our cows. It was around 4 PM, with the sun tracking lower in the sky, sliding drowsily toward sunset—that sacred time we Australians call "beer o'clock."

I'd worked cattle most of my adult life, so separating a bull from the herd on a motorbike was straightforward. After cutting the bull from the herd of cows and forcing him down the boundary fence toward the gate, I decided to slow the pace, knowing he'd relax his trot and walk. As I braked and slowed the bike, the bull also slowed. But then he stopped, turned, tensed his shoulders, narrowed his eyes, and targeted directly at me.

Then, in a split second, the bull put his head down and charged at me—hooves pounding, rocks flying, dust swirling, the ground beneath his feet shuddering with the force of an earthquake. My heart raced. My brain went into escape mode as I attempted a fast, tight U-turn on the bike.

I'd managed to turn halfway around when the bull slammed into me, knocking me off the bike, flipping me into the hard paddock, and turning the tranquil landscape into a dusty tangle of twisted human body and motorbike parts.

I gasped. Beyond the wrecked bike, I spied the bull galloping away from the carnage, storming through the fence, and heading back to his home paddock. I lifted my head and dragged my stunned body to a sitting position. I felt a sudden, excruciating burst of pain at my foot.

That's when I looked down and saw that my right boot, now jammed under the Yamaha's engine, had been ripped away from my foot. My toes stuck out at horrible right angles.

My immediate reaction was to reach out to my disjointed foot, yet I was unable to move my right arm. With my left hand, I reached back to investigate and pulled it back in horror—my entire right shoulder was no longer where it should have been.

As I slumped back in the dirt, panic disoriented me. Waves of pain ripped through me. I fumbled for my phone, but it wasn't there. I scoured my jeans pockets and then the ground. I slammed my fist into the dust, eyes welling with tears. Then I screamed, as hard and loud as I could. But no one could hear me.

Back at the homestead, my wife, Fiona, luckily happened to notice me sprawled on the ground a third of a mile away and grabbed our daughter Brooke to race toward the sound of my screaming. Fiona called Emergency 000, and the ambulance arrived forty minutes later to administer pain relief, but it had no effect. The forty-five-minute drive over the paddock, rocky roads, and finally the highway to the hospital in Newcastle seemed never-ending.

My pain was eventually relieved in the emergency room when I was placed under general anesthetic so the doctors could treat my injuries. I awoke with Fiona and Brooke by my side to learn my toes had been severely dislocated and broken, my shoulder had a severe posterior dislocation—one of the most painful injuries the human body can suffer—and my bicep was torn from the bone, requiring surgery that week and again in a year's time.

I spent ten days in the hospital, followed by two months of recovery at home. The accident affected every aspect of my life: my business and income, my wife and kids, my friends, my health, and my fitness.

I spent the next two years in intense physiotherapy, exercising, stretching, and swimming most mornings in the ocean rock pool at North Narrabeen. This was followed by another two years of Pilates, gym sessions, more exercise, and more swimming. From time to time, I battled post-traumatic stress disorder (PTSD)—intense flashbacks, anxiety, mood dysfunction, intrusive thoughts, and a heightened sense of danger. I felt cut off from people, on edge, and angry. There were mornings when I feared I'd become a prisoner to the unbearable chronic pain and PTSD for the rest of my life.

Looking back, those four years were some of the most challenging of my life. But it gave me the opportunity to give my early-rising strategies the ultimate test. So, as soon as my arm was free of its sling and the cast was taken off my foot, I again set my alarm for 5 AM. My strategy was to use the 5 AM Advantage with the singular goal of making my life better, again.

And it worked—again.

And that's how I know it will work for you, too.

Those years rehabilitating also gave me the opportunity to scrutinize and vastly improve how the strategies are outlined in this book. In the following pages, I share my eighteen-year experiment with waking up at 5 AM and the well-tested strategies I developed to help you discover—or rediscover—your goals and dreams and take specific action to give yourself the best chance of success. By the end of this book, you will be able to fast-track your own journey to whatever you desire.

Then you will have the 5 AM Advantage, too, and be awake to your why.

CHAPTER 1

THE 5 AM MINDSET

The 5 AM Advantage always starts with a split-second decision—to set your alarm for 5 AM. That's it. That's the first step. But it's easier said than done. In this chapter, you learn all about the 5 AM mindset: where it came from, what it is, how to cultivate it, and what it takes to not only make that first decision to wake up early but also continue to do so day after day—for as long as you decide. You also learn how to overcome the obstacles that tend to prevent people from becoming 5 AMers.

THE ORIGINS OF THE 5 AM MINDSET

Mankind has been waking up at first light for millions of years. So, like many of the traits we have carried in our DNA since the dawn of time, waking up early is natural. At first, it may have been out of necessity. There was no artificial light, so it made sense to rise and sleep with the sun. As people started gathering in villages, sleeping in shelters, and using fire, they could stay up past sunset. Still, early humans used a variety of methods—from roosters (as early as 9000 BC) to primitive water alarm clocks (300 BC)—to rise early and start a productive day. From there, alarm clock technology kept improving and never stopped waking early risers.[1]

---

1   Withings, "The History of Waking Up: Humans Edition," *Withings Blog*, August 1, 2014, https://blog.withings.com/2014/08/01/the-history-of-waking-up-how-man-gradually-improved-his -wake-up-experience.

Waking up early has long been considered an advantageous trait. Aristotle (384–322 BC) is believed to have said, "It is well to be up before daybreak, for such habits contribute to health, wealth, and wisdom." This sentiment was repeated in various documented proverbs over the centuries until Benjamin Franklin made famous his version—"Early to bed and early to rise, makes a man healthy, wealthy, and wise"—in his 1732 Poor Richard's Almanack.[2]

Franklin's daily schedule is well documented. He attempted to wake up at 5 AM each day. In the morning, he asked himself the question "What good shall I do today?" and between the hours of 5 AM and 7 AM, he would "contrive [the] day's business and take the resolution of the day; prosecute the present study; and breakfast."[3] What good did it do him? Franklin, famous in his own time, is still revered for his lasting contributions to science, US politics, and civic life.

Those who appreciated the benefits of early rising have truly influenced the world, from George Washington and Thomas Jefferson to more recent early risers such as Nobel Prize winner for literature Toni Morrison, actor Mark Wahlberg, boxing great Muhammad Ali, and my favorite, John Grisham (who has inspired my own writing). In the February 5, 2008, issue of the *San Francisco Chronicle*, Grisham wrote, "The alarm clock would go off at five, and I'd jump in the shower. My office was five minutes away. And I had to be at my desk, at my office, with the first cup of coffee, a legal pad and write the first word at 5:30, five days a week."

The list of famous early risers is long, which has given me great inspiration and motivation to keep at it over the years. And although early rising alone does not guarantee success, a common routine among society's leaders cannot be ignored.

---

2   Benjamin Franklin, *Poor Richard's Almanack* (Waterloo, IA: USC Publishing, 1914), 20.

3   Chris Good, "Picture of the Day: Benjamin Franklin's Daily Schedule," *The Atlantic*, April 20, 2011, https://www.theatlantic.com/politics/archive/2011/04/picture-of-the-day-benjamin-franklins -daily-schedule/237615.

WHAT THE 5 AM MINDSET IS—AND WHAT IT ISN'T

As we see, people throughout history have used the strategy of waking up early to achieve various goals. But I want to be very clear here; this habit is not about waking early to simply work longer, jam more in, or make your day even busier than it already is. It's not about making a fortune while missing out on time with your family and friends, working so hard you lose focus on your own health and fitness, or forgoing the spirit of life that makes us happy. The 5 AM mindset is about becoming the person you want to be.

Waking up at 5 AM should be a habit that reenergizes your desires, reboots your dreams, and reinvents your life, whatever that means to you. Embodying the 5 AM mindset means you believe—to your core—that a better life is necessary, that it must be lived *now*, and that you will achieve it by practicing discipline, persistence, focus, action, and passion toward specific goals. As you will see, the 5 AM mindset puts you in control of your dreams. It makes those dreams sustainable. And it allows you to create a time in the day when *you* are the priority. This is critical because a person with lost or broken dreams is also lost or broken.

WHAT YOU'RE UP AGAINST

Right now, you may be thinking, *Who the hell wants to get up at 5 AM?!* You're right, being a 5 AMer is a challenge. And a 5 AMer must rise to meet that challenge to not only take that first step—setting the alarm for 5 o'clock—but also continue to do so day after day.

Being busy, overworked, and overwhelmed is too often proudly worn like a badge of honor as you battle through your daily slog at work, meet obligations and responsibilities, and struggle head down toward who knows where. And it may seem easier to simply surrender to the grind and abandon earlier dreams than to take massive action in making uncomfortable change.

Fear and discouragement will make you doubt that you can do it. Fear is the voice that undermines your dreams, sabotages your ambitions, and drains your energy for making change. Discouragement is the old failures that hold you back and your resistance to confront the withered heart of your dreams. Together, fear and discouragement immobilize you.

But you must account carefully for what is at stake; stagnation sets in when we live our life from within our comfort zone. The cost of stagnation can be high indeed—loss of income, loss of health, loss of happiness, loss of self-respect, and loss of opportunity. When we lose these, we struggle and weaken. We live not with intention and purpose but rather from one accident to the next. Out of control.

5 AMers are keenly aware of what is at stake and learn to block out the voice of fear and discouragement, to wake up and be free to move toward their goals. How do they block out the negativity? By reframing what *challenge* means to them.

CHALLENGE = PATH TO GROWTH

Many people live their lives trying to avoid difficulties and challenges because they are afraid to fail. In society, we are often taught that failure isn't an option because stories of great success gain the most recognition and stand the test of time. For example, most of us don't learn about the number of times Benjamin Franklin tried and failed; history books tend to emphasize his successful contributions. In more recent times, the media elevates winners to dizzy heights while quickly forgetting those who came behind. At the 2008 Summer Olympics, Jamaican sprinter Usain Bolt catapulted to fame when he won the gold medal and broke his own world record for the 100-meter race. But have you heard of Richard Thompson, the second-place finisher?

The core belicf of a 5 AMer is that the action of stepping up to a challenge is a sign of success—full stop. A 5 AMer knows that action, including the setbacks, will result in personal growth that allows them to take the next step. And the next.

Stepping up to a challenge has become a daily pattern in my life because the benefits have always outweighed the cost of stagnation. I learned this lesson long ago in my childhood when my cousin dared me to jump from a high riverbank into the dark brown waters below.

Staring down from that cliff, I was terrified. My knees shook. Sweat trickled down my neck. *You must be joking!* my brain protested. The older kids were jumping, so I knew it could be done. Still, it stirred up my deepest fears. I discovered that if I stood at the edge, looking down, thinking about the jump—the height, my death, the jagged rocks beneath, my bashed and broken bones—my thoughts fueled that fear into paralysis.

In desperation, my mind found a solution: the decision to jump needed to be made with certainty before I was near the cliff. Then, I would take massive action when approaching the edge by scoping the take-off point to ensure my safe footing for no more than a few seconds and, without any more thought, boldly jump. The process needed to be fluid, fast, and without hesitation, even if my heart was racing. Once I leaped from the riverbank and took flight, my anxiety was instantly released. The hard work was over. Down I plummeted, the wind whistling through my hair, the impact point quickly approaching, until I plunged into the river, where the rushing cold water enveloped me, sucking me under. As my trajectory transitioned from falling to rising beneath the water's surface, an immediate sense of empowerment flooded my mind. For a moment, I relaxed as if drifting in space, taking in the success of the challenge. Yet the real reward came when I gazed up from the water's surface and saw where I had come from, knowing I did it. It felt empowering.

Knowing I could step out of my comfort zone and into the unknown continued to allure me. After college, I challenged myself to leave behind my friends and family and drive into the Australian outback to work on a sheep and cattle station. The harsh heat, soul-crushing isolation, and brutal working hours made the jackarooing experience one of the most enriching and empowering chapters in my life.

Later, I set forth on the challenge of planting trees in Canada, battling black bears, insect plagues, and back-breaking labor. I challenged myself to swim in the freezing waters of the Arctic Ocean, under the never-setting sun of Tuktoyaktuk. And to ride solo on a motorbike in Thailand's Golden Triangle. Why? Because I knew I would remember those experiences for the rest of my life.

Had I instead stagnated and missed any of these opportunities to grow, my life would be different. I honestly believe I would be a different man, a weaker man, with a less rich life. That's what is at stake.

I relished each challenge—pushing past pain, learning to embrace what I fear, gaining a sense of achievement, or even just the satisfaction of trying as best I could no matter the result. Whether in the end I was drenched in sweat and snot or tears and blood matters not. It's about living to my full potential and discovering what my mind and body are capable of.

Confronting and overcoming challenges in life is how we learn and grow. When we misstep, we learn to make a different decision next time. And when we step out of our comfort zones and succeed, it reinforces self-belief; we know we are capable of tackling challenges. And self-belief is the antidote to fear and discouragement. More often than not, when we believe we can do it, we do.

A 5 AM mindset comes in handy when we choose what challenges to confront, but it also helps us overcome unexpected challenges. And life will always throw you unexpected challenges. When I was ten years old, my father was tragically killed in an airplane crash. At the age of thirty-three, I faced the demise of my marriage, the pain of divorce, and the shared custody of my children, ages one, three, and five. Not to mention, being smashed into the ground by the charging bull left me battling major physical injuries and mental trauma that challenges me to this day.

Being grateful and appreciative of how those unexpected challenges lead to growth can be damn hard. For example, after my father's death, my life changed radically, and it's still the greatest challenge I've faced. Yes, it has helped shape who I am today in many positive ways, but fuck that! Having a dad over the past forty years would have been much better. So how can I be grateful for that challenge? How can I appreciate it?

This is extremely hard to answer, and the truth is, in terms of liking it, I can't. But in terms of understanding that it resulted in character traits that have helped me in life, I can. Therefore, a 5 AM mindset simply accepts that good things do come from those challenges. When I accept that any outcome is positive, I also accept that any challenge I face results in growth and benefits my life.

MOTIVATION: 5 AMERS NEED A GOAL

So we know that waking up at 5 AM is not always easy. That's why a key part of the 5 AM mindset is motivation: What is your compelling reason to wake up early tomorrow? What is your primary purpose? What is your goal? What are you going to do? What is your why?

These are important questions—potentially the most important questions—and we return to them again and again in this book. Without a reason to wake up at 5 AM—your why—there is little to no point in doing so.

My reasons to jump out of bed with energy have changed over the years, but I've always had a reason: redirect my business focus, write this book, jog on the beach to stay fit, swim in the freezing pool midwinter to rehabilitate my shoulder, and more. Whether my purpose was to achieve a dream or overcome adversity, my intentions were clear.

The size of the task or label you give it does not matter. If you decide you want to run three miles up the beach, that's great. Call that a goal, a challenge, a desire, or a primary purpose for waking up early. If you achieve the three miles and then decide your next goal is to run a marathon, that may turn into an obsession, or (as we explore in chapter 4) a magnificent obsession.

For now, decide on a goal, no matter its size. Your goal may already be eating at you—because you've been ignoring it—so now is your opportunity to step up to that challenge once and for all. Maybe you will learn a new language. Or organize the notes for that bestseller you want to write. Or search for a new business name online.

Focus on something that gets you excited, that makes your heart soar, and that fuels you with a burning desire. By engaging the 5 AM mindset, ideas will start to ignite and spark. If the ideas haven't sparked or if you know things could be better but aren't exactly sure how, don't worry. Just decide on a small goal that will motivate you to wake up tomorrow morning. I promise that action will motivate you toward bigger goals. I talk more about how the energy of both action and motivation will help you achieve everything you challenge yourself to in chapter 8.

REMEMBER, IT'S PRACTICE

The morning after my breaking point with the piglet, when my alarm buzzed at 5 AM, I had a simple goal: to wake and get to the beach to exercise. With the moon above me, as the first light crept toward the horizon, my feet touched down on the cold sand and the wind bathed my face in sea air. My eyes watered with tears as my overwhelmed world instantly stabilized. I took another step in the sand, then another. I had disrupted my old pattern. I no longer felt chained to my broken life. I had found the catalyst for freedom, for real self-improvement.

Becoming a 5 AMer starts with an action: setting your alarm for 5 AM. But simply taking one action isn't good enough. If that were the case, Tiger Woods could turn up to golf tournaments and win every time he tees up. A 5 AMer must practice the action every morning, every week, every month, over and over again. Equally, we must practice discipline, practice persistence, practice focus, and find passion—concepts I outline in the following chapters. That is the purpose of the 5 AM Advantage; it's the practice of living a better life, a more abundant life.

I was not a 5 AMer because I woke up early one morning. I became a 5 AMer because I continued to practice every day. I practiced waking up early, I practiced my new mindset, and I practiced making my new routine enjoyable (because it wasn't always). Whether I was overwhelmed or in control didn't matter—I practiced. Empowered or overpowered—I practiced. In good health or poor health, happy or depressed—I practiced. Practice was the difference. Practice is what helped me take *advantage* of my time. With practice, I was empowered to tackle any strategy and ignore any distraction that might sabotage my efforts. With practice, I adapted and evolved. I have been adapting and evolving toward my best self for the past eighteen years. There are no overnight fixes or cures. Self-improvement is an endurance race, and there is always room to grow.

With practice, you will succeed.

I promise.

FAST-TRACK TIPS FOR RISING EARLY

1. Organize what you'll need in the morning. For example, if my goal is to go to the gym, then I will have 100 percent packed my gym bag and have all my clothes ready before I climb into bed. That way, I'm not banging around in the dark, delaying my action.

2. Next, have a conversation with yourself about your goal. Remind yourself how much better your life will be when you practice the 5 AM mindset each morning. As you visualize, stand tall and proud, with your chest out and chin raised as if you've just achieved your wildest dream. Feel the blood pump. Feel the energy flow. Enjoy it. You're a 5 AMer now, and you're working on your goals! You're about to step up to a great challenge that will change your life. Please don't downplay this. Your decision to master waking up early will alter everything.

3. When the day ends, go to bed early. Organize your evening so you have time to wind down for an early sleep. I'm usually in bed by 9:30 PM, and it's lights out at 10:00 PM. If you're a night owl, don't overthink this. After a few days of rising at 5:00 AM, going to sleep early will be easy!

4. Finally, remember that it's practice. If you don't always wake up as intended, don't give up. By the end of this book, you'll have everything you need to achieve success—I promise.

CHAPTER 2

THE 5 AM ADVANTAGE

I f you've made it this far, you've decided you are ready to move from simply having a *habit* of waking up at 5 AM to *taking advantage* of waking up at 5 AM. The difference in a nutshell? Intention. My master strategy—the 5 AM Advantage—helps foster that intention in you. This strategy includes several supporting strategies, tools, and rules that I've developed over the eighteen years I've been a practicing 5 AMer. This chapter walks you through the most important concepts, so you are ready to dive deep in the chapters that follow.

A NEW SELF-IMPROVEMENT STRATEGY

I was obsessed with self-improvement for years before I developed the 5 AM Advantage. Reading the biographies of high achievers who helped shape the world motivated my appetite to learn more. On a quest to find a better life, I immersed myself in self-help books, seminars, and the strategies of personal growth experts. I read Napoleon Hill's iconic book, *Think and Grow Rich*, in 1991, in the back of a VW Kombi van, driving through the Alaskan wilderness. I was awakened to the possibilities of living a bigger life. I dug into the books, tapes, and CDs of other motivational masters such as Dale Carnegie, Zig Ziglar, Tony Robbins, Eckhart Tolle, Wallace D. Wattles, and many others whose experience allowed me to think bigger and make self-improvement compulsory.

However, although their books, lectures, and programs delivered potentially life-changing insights, I always found it easier to be educated than to physically put those lessons into practice. I found that in a busy life, the influence of these master motivators was compromised and the impulse of self-improvement was temporary, easily pushed aside and quickly forgotten. Before I knew it, I was back on the never-ending treadmill of *doing, doing, doing* without insight or clear direction. I was busy *being busy*. After all, I was working hard to build a business and family. Soon, I was back to where I started—again. And that was disappointing. It was exhausting. That is the reason I started my own search for answers. I needed to find my own path to self-mastery.

I didn't need to completely reinvent the wheel. After all, those gurus had dedicated their lives to helping others live better, and they had a lot of great tools and strategies to learn. But I needed an edge, an advantage, or something these other coaches had missed. I needed a strategy that made sure any chosen path to self-improvement worked. To do this, my strategy needed to be strongly associated with early rising to guarantee that it came first and would be placed ahead of the rest, before the busyness of my day.

In chapter 1, you learn that the physical action of waking up at 5 AM is critical because it acts as a catalyst (something that causes a sudden event or change) because it disrupts your stagnated routine. However, many people wake up early every day to live wretched lives. Therefore, equally important to the catalyst—waking up at 5 AM—is the event or change that follows. Could I figure out a way to ensure that the change was positive, effective, and sustainable? After years of pounding the sand along the beach, swimming laps in the rock pool before sunrise, arriving at work before my staff, and researching, learning, and practicing, I finally observed and defined what that change must be. It must be *intentional*. And thus the 5 am Advantage was born: a strategy to help you create intentional change during the first one or two hours of your day.

Figure 2.1 represents the steps involved in the 5 AM Advantage, steps that will help you be intentional about your 5 AM habit as a catalyst to make a change and live your life as best you can. The remainder of the chapter previews each step.

Figure 2.1: The 5 AM Advantage

THE WAKE-UP CALL

When you have goals that feel out of reach, dreams that have slipped through your fingers, or a life that is passing by without control, you must figure out why. On the graphic, the outer ring enclosing all other parts is the wake-up call. This is the first step of the strategy. Think of it as the outer skin that must be peeled away to reveal the truth.

Life often prompts the wake-up call, an alert that something isn't right and that you need to fix it. Sometimes, we are forced to stop in our tracks—we have a health scare or a health crisis, someone passes, a relationship falls apart, we lose a job, we hit rock bottom, or we experience a breaking point. My breaking point was the day I found myself wrestling a piglet on my forty-second birthday instead of enjoying the day off at home with my family. When something in your life is amiss, you may feel overwhelmed with stress, deeply unhappy, or lost. And you may ask yourself, *How did I get here?*

That question is key. Becoming aware that something is not right is great, but it's only the first part of the wake-up call because we too often bury those feelings, distract ourselves, and keep our minds busy on other things. So, if you want to truly live a better life, you must engage with the reasons behind why you're in this less-than-ideal place. You must answer the bigger question: Why did I get here?

This involves introspection: taking a deep look at your life, discovering why you ended up off your path, and figuring out who your authentic self really is. Because without knowing *who* you really are, it is impossible to know where you need to go. Understanding yourself gives you direction. It sets you free. I developed a tool called the *accidental life journal* to help you with this introspection. You use it in chapter 3 to confront your true self and track how you got to where you are today so you can awaken to your why.

GOALS AND MAGNIFICENT OBSESSIONS

In the graphic's center is a bull's-eye that says goals and magnificent obsessions. To make massive positive changes to your life, you need a target—the goal you want to hit. Sometimes, your goal is a smaller part of a larger goal or a goal of more importance. Often, a goal evolves into a magnificent obsession—something that is so critical that you *must* achieve it. Other times, you know from the beginning that it is a must-do, and you will become magnificently obsessed with successfully achieving it.

When I started waking up early each morning, my goal was to walk over to the beach and start jogging, swimming, or working out at the gym. But my magnificent obsession was to build a better life, which included being fit, healthy, and grateful for living life as best I could. At other times, my goal was to write. But my magnificent obsession was to finish a great book, no matter how long it took.

Deciding to become magnificently obsessed with a goal is a mindset strategy that allows you to bring something that is a "must" to a higher level of consciousness. This is powerful because whenever an object we desire is front of mind, it is acted on with urgency and certainty. When you are magnificently obsessed, you know without a shadow of a doubt that you will do whatever it takes to successfully achieve your goal, and with that certainty, you will. I'm not a natural writer, but I have a magnificent obsession with writing a great book. You will be the judge of that, but I know there are thousands of books that have never made it past a thought. So I achieved success, all because a goal became a magnificent obsession.

In chapter 4, you learn how to identify goals and how to become magnificently obsessed when required.

THE GOAL ACTIVATORS

The second ring of the 5 AM Advantage graphic is made up of five goal activators: discipline, persistence, focus, action, and passion. Each goal activator works in concert with the others—leading to and resulting from each other—creating forward momentum. This momentum is the energy that spurs you along. Activated goals progress toward success, and inactivated goals lose energy, increasing the likelihood of failure. Let's take a brief look at each of the five goal activators.

It starts with *discipline*, the first goal activator. Nothing is possible without discipline. It's the self-control you need to work toward your goal and stay on your path without straying, no matter the temptation, challenge, or doubts that come your way. In chapter 5, you learn to master discipline with my ten rules for the disciplined 5 AMer.

Persistence is the second goal activator. The goals you aim to achieve and the life you dream of living are yours for the taking, but it requires persistence—the ability to keep working toward your goal over the long term—and plenty of it! Persistence is evolutionary, transformational, and all empowering. Every day that you wake at 5 AM moves you one step closer to achieving success. Day by day, you persist. And with the grit of persistence, you succeed, even when obstacles temporarily slow you down or knock you off course. (Persistence is what makes the slowdown, or even a pause, temporary.) In chapter 6, you learn about neuroplasticity, a concept that helps you understand persistence on a deeper level.

Focus is the third goal activator. You have focus when you direct your attention toward a clear vision—in this case, what you desire is to live a better life. Focus attracts you to all you require to succeed. Focus pulls you toward your higher self. Focus prevents distractions. Focus is the difference between intense purpose and vague hope. In chapter 7, you learn how to use tools that help you focus, including mind mapping and the 80/20 principle.

The fourth goal activator is *action*. Action is a thing done. It's movement. It's what you do and how you behave to achieve your goal over time. You must take action every day. When you take action, your fitness, speed, expertise, skills, productivity, and returns on effort increase. In chapter 8, you learn how to create an MO statement, which helps you take action toward achieving goals that remain relevant and front of mind, have a deadline, and align with the new life you have decided to live.

Passion is the fifth goal activator. Passion is an intense, driving, all-consuming feeling or conviction. All you do in life must be powered by passion. Passion is the rocket fuel that drives success. You need to be fired up about waking early and achieving your dream. Acting with passion makes life exciting. It floods us with energy. Passion makes us courageous. Passion makes us lead. Passion makes us magnificent. In chapter 9, you learn how passion manifests and how to harness it.

GOAL ACTIVATOR SYNERGY

Together, the five goal activators create what I call 5 AMer synergy, which is represented by the inner cog that connects all the activators and surrounds the goals and magnificent obsessions in the 5 AM Advantage graphic (figure 2.1). The word *synergy* encapsulates an adage that you've probably heard before: the whole is greater than the sum of its parts. The goal activators (the parts) combine to create the unstoppable, self-sustaining energy (the whole) you need to hit your target.

This concept is key. The goal activators represent admirable qualities, but in isolation, none of them are strong enough to get you where you want to go. This is why we (yep, me included) have fallen short of goals in the past.

Each activator needs the other four to fully resonate, and you need all five of them—the powerful combination—to achieve success. In other words:

- *Discipline* requires persistence, focus, passion, and action.
- *Persistence* requires discipline, focus, passion, and action.
- *Focus* requires passion, action, persistence, and discipline.
- *Action* requires persistence, discipline, focus, and passion.
- *Passion* requires action, persistence, discipline, and focus.

The five goal activators are available to you each morning. If my goal is to exercise at the beach at 5 AM, then yes, I need discipline when the alarm goes off, but I empower that with passion (how good it will feel to watch the sunrise over the ocean), and persistence (every time I do this, it gets easier as I'm changing who I am), and focus (on how incredible I feel after my exercise), and action (stop thinking and get yourself out of bed—momentum creates motivation). First goal of the day—achieved!

This is the 5 AM Advantage, a master strategy for achieving the goals you need to live your best life. Now, it's time to start enacting the strategy. Our first stop is your wake-up call.

CHAPTER 3

THE WAKE-UP CALL

The truth is you gotta find something within!
And that's gotta push you. And that's gotta elevate you.
And that's gotta drive you. And that's gotta move you.
And when you find out what your why is, . . . you don't hit snooze
no more. When you find your why, you find a way to make it happen.

—Eric Thomas, "This Is Why I Grind"[4]

I f you're reading this book, you likely have already experienced the first part of the wake-up call—something in life has stopped you dead in your tracks and prompted you to ask, "How did I get here?" However, it's not enough to just ask the question. That's only the beginning. To complete the first step of the 5 AM Advantage, you must *answer* this question: "Why did I get here?" That means looking inward. And that's what this chapter is all about.

But be prepared: this chapter challenges you to dig deep and write an important document—perhaps the most important document you will ever write! Writing this document may be uncomfortable, but it will enable you to observe your life in totality and gain an understanding of the decisions that led you to where you are today and, most importantly, *who* you are

---

4   See the full talk at https://www.youtube.com/watch?v=tVYxvNLsRvs.

today. It's called the *accidental life journal*. And whatever happens in your life, after writing this journal, you will be empowered by one thing: your truth. Let's begin!

WHY OUR PERSONAL TRUTHS MATTER

Over the years, many of us have suppressed our personal truths as we try to survive day to day. Sometimes, we feel we must shut down our authentic selves to work hard, meet deadlines, be good parents, make more money, pay the mortgage, create relationships—you name it. Often, we forget what our truth even is. Overworked, overburdened, and overwhelmed, we suddenly feel untethered from our true purpose, if we ever knew what that was to begin with.

Before we know it, life feels like it is driving us, instead of the other way around. And that's what leads to dreams deferred, lost ambition, feelings of stagnation, and an ever-present sense that life should be somehow better. Remember that your truth is your North Star—it helps you find your direction, control, and purpose. Without it, your life is at risk of being lived unintentionally, often as a series of accidents that leave a trail of unachieved goals in their wake.

THE ACCIDENTAL LIFE

Here's the thing: when you're living what I call an accidental life—one that is left up to chance and not powered by intention, purpose, and direction— you're likely already lost. You might not know where or when you started veering off the path you intended to be on. You might not even know what the path is because you might not know what you want, what drives you, what gives you direction, or what is standing in your way.

This is partly because, on one level, an accidental life appears to work. Random events add to the mystery, beauty, and flavor of life. This randomness creates variety, and variety makes the world an interesting place. We accidentally arrive at new destinations, work in accidental jobs, overcome accidental problems, and seemingly find accidental direction. Yet, in many other ways, it's a tragedy because it results in the kind of consequences that leave us unfulfilled: lost time, careless mistakes, bad decisions, misspent passions, squandered ambitions, wasted opportunities, and broken dreams.

We only have so much time here on earth, and every minute we spend *re*acting to an accidental step is a minute we're not *acting* to achieve our dreams and goals. That can lead to regret. We can feel disoriented, overwhelmed, and out of control. That said, we are never going to have total control of our lives; that's an impossibility. However, it's essential to fight hard to control what we can and set ourselves up for the probability of success. Our health and fitness, happiness, love, wealth, dreams, passion, and adventure must not be left to chance alone.

The other challenge is that we tend to avoid facing the truth, we learn to hide feelings of regret caused by unachieved plans and goals, and we don't take responsibility for them. We simply ignore the fact that we're allowing factors around us and within us to dictate our journey in life. I kept this truth from myself for decades.

It was too easy for me to avoid the truth. Why? Because my life wasn't *totally* out of control. I wasn't bankrupt, alcoholic, violent, manically depressed, or apparently self-destructive. Crashing and burning more dramatically may have alerted me earlier. Remember, I was busy running a successful business, widely recognized as the leader in my field. I had a great wife and four wonderful children with a house by the beach and a farm in the country. I was reasonably fit and healthy. By many accounts, life appeared to be good.

Except, I didn't *feel* good. I wasn't living an authentic life. I was forty-something years old and wrangling farm animals for school children. That life was someone else's dream, not mine, and I had spent many years of my life living it. (Even as I write this, I feel tension in my gut.) It felt out of whack with where I thought I should be. And, eventually, I couldn't ignore the questions that kept popping into my head: What happened to the boy that grew up into this man? What happened to his dreams, ambitions, and desires? Why had I allowed them to fade? Will I ever truly live the life I desire? Am I good enough? Am I *not* good enough? Who *am* I? And yes—*why did I get here?*

I couldn't answer any of those questions, at least not right away. I couldn't see the forest for the trees, which happens in a busy life. But my wake-up call told me it was time to pause and reflect. Some kind of intuition told me that writing out my life story might help. At the time, I didn't know what to expect. But every day, I woke up at 5 AM and set aside an hour or two to focus on my life. And I wrote it down. I called it my accidental life journal, and it turned out to be one of the most enlightening periods of my life.

My accidental life journal helped me see when and where I had made wrong turns or was forced off a path and why I had started feeling so full of remorse. It helped me understand my authentic self and decide where I wanted to go. That's why I now recommend that everyone complete an accidental life journal as part of their wake-up call. To start on the right foot, it's imperative we answer that all-important question—Why did I get here?—and the journal will help you do that.

THE ACCIDENTAL LIFE JOURNAL

To write your accidental life journal, you must stop being "too busy" to question the direction of your life. You must pause and take stock by looking back over the years already lived to gain an understanding of the forces that have pushed you or influenced your actions and decisions, right up to reading this book, at this very moment, today. Then, with an improved understanding of who you are, you can make intentional decisions that will direct your future years so you can live a better life.

We all have a story. Often, our story has been fictitiously fabricated by an ego that's trying hard to interoperate with the world—more accurately, by an ego competing for control. As you read later in this chapter, my story revealed a lifelong perception of not belonging, being out of place, not good enough, unequipped, forever regretful, and forever grieving. I felt unworthy and unqualified, and this estrangement was all-consuming. No wonder I felt sad.

Your accidental life journal will reveal your obstacles, insecurities, self-limitations, self-sabotage, and much more—all uniquely derived from your personal story. In other words, it will reveal your truth. And your truth will empower you for the rest of your life.

Journaling allows you to look at your life through a new lens. Instead of simply reacting, you will learn how to *act*, how to steer your ship toward horizons of your own choosing. When you're in control, you don't regret as much. You breathe better because you know and accept who you are and why you arrived at this moment in time. You stand tall, confident in your chosen path forward. You live in the now.

Here's the most important thing to keep in mind: to answer "Why did I get here?," you must be authentic with yourself as you write. If you don't engage with this exercise genuinely—if you never reach below the surface—you will likely continue with your busy, unfocused, and undirected life, allowing events to take control and push you along an impulsive existence, one that forces you to *re*act to accident after accident.

How to Write Your Accidental Life Journal

To start, set your alarm for 5 AM and set aside one to two hours each morning for writing your life story—from the earliest memory to the present day. The length and format you choose don't matter. What's critical is that you take time to carefully listen to your inner self—your *self* is ready to be heard.

Generally speaking, as long as you give yourself fully to this process with total immersion while writing, you'll receive all the benefits of your accidental life journal. Don't force an answer to, "Why did I get here?" At this stage, simply allow a truthful and honest conversation with yourself. And when the moment is right, triggered by an event or series of events you write down, the answer will be revealed. The depth of this conversation will be both new and intense. Listening to your inner voice truthfully and honestly will also be emotional and confronting. As the answer becomes apparent, allow your mind and body to react without suppression. You're having this conversation with yourself, and the answer is for you and you alone. No one in the entire world need ever read this journal.

You don't need to be limited by rules or structure—every journal is totally unique—but here are some tips to consider before you begin:

- *Don't worry about how long it takes.* How long the journal takes will vary from person to person. It took me more than a month to complete mine, which included writing most mornings for an hour or two.

- *Break down your life story into chapters.* Depending on your age, break your story down into digestible periods of time. I chose to use periods of decades.

- *Start each period with the events that took place (facts).* This can be done as bullet points or in prose, but the key is to get the facts on paper first, without your interpretation.

- *Conclude each period with your reflections (thoughts).* This is when you have that deep conversation with your inner self to write down how you thought at the time, how you feel now, how the event influenced your life (was it positive or negative), and so on. Give all thoughts the freedom to transfer from your inner self to the page.

- *Allow yourself to jump between writing out the facts and your reflections.* Often, while writing down the facts of an event, a conversation with your inner self will begin. Go to the reflections section for that event period immediately and nurture the conversation. This is where the truth is revealed—let it flow naturally. You may need to repeat this back and forth until the entire period is complete.

- *Enlist helpers to fill in the blanks.* You may not remember all the details of certain situations, especially from when you were young. I talked to my mother about events that had faded from memory.

- *Don't censor yourself.* Write down all your thoughts as they come; don't censor them. This is called stream of consciousness writing and is when the magic happens! From this subconscious experience, you will gain the gift of wisdom.

- *Write in total silence.* It's not the time to get creative with music playing in the background. This is the time to listen deeply from within. You have been ignoring this voice for way too long—stop all distractions.

- *Allow your emotions to ignite.* Passion, sadness, sorrow, grief, elation, disgust, anger, contempt, fear, self-hostility, shame, guilt, joy—you may experience all of these and more. Don't suppress them. Your emotions may have been bottled up for years. Give yourself permission and privacy to experience them.

- *Seek help if needed.* If you feel you need to talk to a professional about issues that arise while journaling, please do so.

Prompts

If you feel ready to get started on your accidental life journal, you can start immediately. For those of you who need a little bit more direction, I've created a series of prompts to help get the words flowing. However, don't feel hampered or restricted by these prompts. When you feel compelled to go in your own direction, do so.

1. What is your earliest memory? What are the most vivid memories from your childhood?
2. What is your family history? What kind of relationship did you have with your parents and siblings as a child? Teen? Adult?
3. What does your name mean? Were you named after anything or anyone?
4. Where have you lived?
5. What was the best part of growing up? The hardest?
6. Where did you go to school?
7. Who have been your closest friends in your life? Have any of them remained constant?
8. When have you felt most alive? What made you feel so alive during those times?
9. What accomplishments have made you feel most proud in your life?

10. What events made you feel the most embarrassed or ashamed? What happened and how did you deal with these feelings?

11. Have you ever had to face challenges alone? What were they and how did you overcome them?

12. Who have been the greatest loves in your life? What do you appreciate the most about those relationships? Regret the most?

13. When did you first live independently from your family? What was the best part of that experience? The hardest part?

14. What kind of jobs have you had in your life? What was your favorite one and what did you like most about it?

15. What is one memory that you never want to forget? Why was it so memorable?

MY ACCIDENTAL LIFE JOURNAL

To best prepare you for writing your accidental life journal, I believe sharing some notes from my own is appropriate. My actual journal is more detailed than this, but it should give you some idea of what yours might look like. While knowing my life story will give you a deeper connection to my journey, the strategies that helped me greatly through this process are not addressed here. I have purposely left those notes out so we can look at the strategies in detail over the chapters that follow.

Decade One: 1965–1974

1965: Born in the country town of Deniliquin, in the Riverina region of New South Wales, Australia. I lived on an eighty-eight-thousand-acre sheep station, forty miles from town, with my mum, dad, two older sisters, and about eight staff (cook, jackaroos, etc.). Dad was the property's head manager and worked hard. I recall the blistering heat of summer, playing in the vast homestead gardens with my sisters, and rescuing chicks that had fallen to the ground from their nests.

1970: The station was sold; we moved to a beautiful horse and cattle property three hundred miles away near the village of Collector. I completed kindergarten and started my first school year with only twelve students in the entire school. Some days, we wouldn't have a teacher, and we had to rely on a two-way radio for lessons. There was a rope bridge crossing the river near our homestead. This was exciting to cross as it swayed and rocked from side to side. I learned to ride a Shetland pony—a naughty pony, often bolting across the paddock and throwing me off, once over a fence.

1971: Dad lost his job. Until he could find another farm to work, we moved to a small apartment in Sydney's Northern Beaches neighborhood, where I attended school. We soon moved again to a nearby suburb, where I loved to collect silkworms from the backyard tree. Yet again, I started at a new school.

1972: Dad started a new job, managing a cattle property near the town of Cootamundra, 250 miles to the south of Sydney. The homestead was massive; the yard contained a large swimming pool with sweeping views over the majestic green paddocks—nothing like the outback of Deniliquin! Dad gave me some homing pigeons; eagles kept attacking them as they flew back to their coop after release. Strange as it now seems, there was a polar bear skin on the sitting room floor, complete with its head. I loved falling asleep on that cozy rug in front of the fire. I felt safe. Then, in late 1972, Dad lost his job again, and we moved 150 miles to another small apartment in the town of Albury, probably because my nanna (Dad's mum) lived nearby. I finished first class (for the second time) and remember exploring Nanna's garage, where I found Grandpa's war uniform and kit.

1973: We moved 150 miles south to a cattle property near the town of Yea in the state of Victoria. Dad gave me my first horse, Blue Boy, as well as my first dog, Rusty. The three of us became best friends. I'd help Dad with the cattle on horseback, riding into the hills. I loved watching him pull calves from cows who had trouble birthing. We'd kick the football (Australian Rules football) together in the open space between the homestead and the stables. I spent a lot of time by myself in the outdoors, fishing in the shade of a willow tree. Farm life was wonderful.

Decade One Reflections

Writing an accidental life journal for my first decade was challenging! The order and reason for some events had become unclear and faded with my memories. What was clear is that those early years were totally determined by Dad's work. As a result, we moved seven times, and I attended eight different schools. Being the new kid in class was hard. Even today, when faced with unfamiliar situations, I can feel unsure and shy.

Growing up on large, rural properties was an adventure filled with outdoor excitement, animals, exploration, and good old-fashioned fun. I forged a strong love of the land and a connection with animals. Even though Dad was busy, he found time to do father and son stuff, such as ride horses together or just kick the football around.

To understand why we moved so many times, I dug deeper, asking questions of my mum. My father was a hard worker and an excellent farm manager, but his diplomatic skills with the city-based owners of the farms fell short on occasion. His inability to compromise or negotiate may have been a problem—but to what extent I will never know. After a lifetime of placing my dad high on a pedestal, acknowledging his shortcomings was at first disappointing but not so bad with reflection. Now I better understand his feelings of stress, frustration, and overwhelm.

One thing is certain: the love of the land was definitely in my blood!

Decade Two: 1975–1984

1975: Dad fell out with the property owner; we moved again. This time, he started a farm management company in our hometown of Deniliquin. Blue Boy lived on one of the properties Dad managed. Regularly, I'd fly with Dad in his single-engine Piper Cherokee, which was needed to cover the large distances. A few times, he gave me control of the joystick, and he pretended I was in charge. I loved those trips.

1976: At the start of our second year back at Deniliquin, I was sitting in the classroom when there was a knock on the door. It was Dad's business partner, who talked quietly to my teacher before I was asked to get my things.

Driving home, he told me the horrible news; Dad's plane crashed that morning, and he had not survived. I remember the cars parked outside our house. Inside, friends filled the home, supporting Mum and my sisters. Because of the number of people, I needed to escape to my bedroom to be alone. It was all so surreal. *When is Dad really coming home?* I wondered. My world had been rocked; the sadness was overwhelming. I was confused. My family was falling apart before me, and my life would never be the same.

Later that year, my nanna died. They say she was grief-stricken and depressed after the loss of her son. Then, my best friend's little sister Jenny was killed when her horse bolted under a tree limb. Their family was now going through the devastation that was still so raw to ours.

1977: Mum decided it would be best to move to Sydney to give me a better education. I attended sixth class at the local primary school on Sydney's North Shore and started Scouts, which I loved.

1978: I started secondary school at a local high school but, halfway through the first term, changed schools to attend a private boy's school, which reduced its fees on compassionate grounds, since I had moved from the country and lost my father. Knox Grammar School had over a thousand students, all formally dressed in strict uniforms, including boater hats and blazers. The teachers were referred to as *masters* and addressed as "sir." The headmaster enforced discipline with the cane. The main sports were rugby in the winter and cricket during the summer, both of which I played. I was also in the swim squad, spending many mornings following the black line in the cold water. Finally, there was the compulsory Australian Army Cadets, in which I became a corporal.

1980: Met my first real girlfriend. Mum also bought a forty-acre block of land seventy-five miles north of Sydney. We spent lots of time working at clearing the bush with a chainsaw and shovel so she could grow flowers to sell at the markets. I found this work difficult for my age, yet always managed to push on.

1981: I got drunk for the first time. A strong social life, parties, and binge drinking were the new normal.

1983: I graduated from high school.

1984: I started a bachelor's degree in business at Hawkesbury Agricultural College (Western Sydney University), living on campus, where my binge-drinking experience was celebrated.

Decade Two Reflections

The second decade of my life is still extremely raw. Writing this part of the journal upset me greatly, and I cried many times. But I pushed on.

At first, I decided that my childhood had ended in 1976, at the age of ten, when my dad died. Further reflection changed this conclusion. It became clearer that this wasn't the end of my childhood but rather the end of that golden period when we are protected from the harsh realities of life. I was no longer oblivious to adversity and pain. I was acutely aware of it. There was tragedy; there was complete sadness; it was out of my control. Dad was dead! Nothing could change that. I even prayed for God's help, but He was silent.

I pushed on through tears and pain, trying to recall the year after my dad's death; it remains lost in a blur of grief. I remember my schoolteacher being kind but cannot remember riding my bike or playing with friends as I once had. I do remember thinking that Dad would walk through the front door any day and that he'd been living a parallel life with another family somewhere. Over the years, I kept an eye out for him, but he never returned.

A strange thing happened to me while writing this part of the journal. I often felt removed from the story. It was as if the narrative was about someone else, some other little boy. This separation allowed me to understand what I had gone through from the perspective of my present adult self. This was new and fresh. My forty-year-old self was understanding and giving unconditional love to that boy. I was comforting myself. I had empathy in its purest form for that little boy. I wanted to hug him. In my mind, from my new perspective, I did—it felt *great*.

Looking back, the deaths of my father, nanna, and friend Jenny, and this shift from living in the country to life in Sydney, were nothing short of traumatic. How could anyone let that happen to that boy? To *me*?

After many chats with Mum, I have come to respect the decisions she made. Being a single parent, she faced her own uncertainty and trauma. As I continued to write, I understood that Mum and my sisters were also damaged. We all did our best to adapt. In the end, I enjoyed my typical middle-class adolescence. There was, however, always a deeper sadness, and I clearly used alcohol to dampen the pain. My self-medication was regularly out of control, and I was always the boy who passed out at parties. I remember loving that state of mind-bending, as it temporarily set me free. Sadly, it often ended with me bawling my eyes out and breaking down in front of my friends before passing out.

This part of the journal allowed me to see why I fell in love for the first time. My girlfriend was a great comfort during this period, but what made her irresistible was that our relationship offered me a complete alternative life to escape into. I was best friends with her brother; her mother was abundant with love and affection; and her father was a kind-hearted man I looked up to, who showed genuine interest in what I had to say and planned to do. All these things seemed absent in my own home life. How could I not fall in love with this package?

The final year of my second decade is when I started university. Hawkesbury Agricultural College back in the '80s was a wild place to be "educated." Its social scene allowed me to drink harder than ever without any apparent care for my own health. I look back at those years with pain, and I feel sad for the little boy who was (it's obvious now) crying out for help. But nobody answered.

Decade Three: 1985–1994

1985–1986: College life. College was great, but having a girlfriend separate from that life was hard. I broke off our relationship, but a couple of months later, we got back together. I finished college, graduating at the end of the year.

1987: Jackaroo on a 56,000-acre sheep and cattle station back in the wide-open plains of my birthplace in the Riverina. I quickly picked up the skills of working on a large property. I also learned how working hard was a great reason to play even harder, and my college "drinking degree" placed me in excellent form. I trained for and completed the Hay, Hell to Booligal Endurance Ride. Mum moved from Sydney back to the country, on a small rural block in Kangaroo Valley.

1988: My boss asked me to stay on as a jackaroo with an eye toward becoming manager of one of the company's large properties. Instead, I declined, leaving to use my business degree to become a property valuer with the NSW State Bank (Rural Bank) while living at Tamworth. I became a well-regarded valuer with an excellent rapport with the local farmers, who appreciated my farming experience and country heritage.

1989: My girlfriend moved in with me, and we started taking things seriously. We purchased a few acres on the edge of town and were married. My work, however, transferred me to the coastal town of Coffs Harbour, so we moved. My new boss was at the end of his career, determined to hang on to old work attitudes and draconian ideas; over time, this made work unbearable. I loved to go surfing in the mornings (and sometimes when I should have been working) and learned to scuba dive.

1990: At the end of the year, I'd endured enough office politics and decided to take six months off work to travel with my wife.

1991: In the New Year, we traveled to New Zealand, the United States, Mexico, and Canada. I resigned from the bank over the phone, so we could continue working in Canada. Then, we traveled separately. I went to British Columbia, Northern Canada, and Alaska. I bought a guitar, read Napoleon Hill's *Think and Grow Rich*, and wrote movie scripts. Eventually, we met up again in London, but she quickly returned home to be with her family. We were having relationship problems and decided we needed a break. I stayed in London to work for another three months without her.

1992: After fifteen months of travel, including riding around Thailand on a motorbike, I returned home. My wife and I had reconciled, and I was warmly welcomed home. To earn some money, I decided to use my jackarooing experience to take a group of farm animals to schools, teaching children about life on a farm. This was my first business venture to pay off our debts before traveling around Australia and finding a place to settle down for the long term. I also took courses in screenwriting and film production—a dream since my travels in Canada.

1993: Nine months after I returned home, our daughter Jess was born. Being a father was awesome.

Decade Three Reflections

Decade three highlights my accidental life. Writing and rereading this journal is like watching a train wreck in slow motion. At times, it was hard for me to understand the thought processes of my twenty-something-year-old self.

I did enjoy college, and I'm sure my business degree was beneficial to my future ventures. Much of college, however, was not about tertiary education. It was about the culture of binge drinking and partying. I was disciplined enough to find time to study, but I found little interest in balance sheets, law, statistics, or building codes.

Graduation marked the end of that era. My return to the bush for a year of jackarooing was a huge challenge, but of all that I have done to this day, jackarooing has come the most naturally. I found something I was good at and passionate about—working on the land. I earned a reputation for being reliable, honest, and valuable. I fell in love with life on the station, and when I was given the opportunity to stay, a powerful sense of achievement came over me. I felt like a man. I could follow in my dad's footsteps.

But I didn't. This was a misstep. At twenty-four, I thought it was important to use my degree and start my professional career. My dad's farm management career had been hard on our family, and that influenced my decision. I now see that I missed my calling. I would never experience that love for a job again.

Being a rural valuer never felt right or authentically me. Conversations about foreclosing on farmers were too hard to swallow. I felt sick in the guts every Sunday night, knowing I would be back in their world the next morning.

Travel was an escape. Although it helped me bond with my wife at first, independent travel allowed me the freedom to grow. I was happy to adventure, and it gave me many moments of self-reflection and inspiration. By the time I joined my wife in London, we had drifted far apart. In a moment of clarity, we split up, but then we got back together when I returned to Australia.

Looking back, I can see this was another misstep that happened because of my vulnerabilities. The loneliness of being solo in London refreshed the pain from my childhood. On my return, I easily yielded to her desire to start a family and settle down. Our financial situation was not good. Journaling helped me realize that I primarily started Kindifarm for financial reasons, not out of passion.

I can now see the unstable foundations that were laid, and the next chapter of my accidental life as a father, husband, and entrepreneur began, which propelled me for the next twenty years. The truth is, I had no plan. I made each life-altering decision in this decade on the run, without understanding their consequences. And I was so busy, I never took the time to see that my accidental life was running its own course.

Decade Four: 1995–2004

1995: Kindifarm grew, and plans for traveling were forgotten as I was occupied with family, business, and entrepreneurship. We bought a house in Narrabeen and began renovating it ourselves. Our son Ollie was born, and though I was busy running Kindifarm, I always rushed home to help with the kids. I started a second business operated under the umbrella of Kindifarm called Ponies for Parties. The name said it all.

1997: Our third child, Oscar, was born. We were extremely busy with work, children, and home renovations. We sold our house to upgrade to a larger home with good potential to renovate. A feeling of being overwhelmed started creeping in.

1998: I was busy, stressed, overwhelmed, unhappy, confused, and out of control. The marriage broke up again, this time resulting in divorce. I relocated Kindifarm to a larger property, requiring total development of vacant acreage to specifically suit the requirements of my business.

1999: I buried myself in working on the newly developed land. I started a third business, Kindifarm Horse Agistment, for boarding horses. I then started a fourth business, My Paddock Parking, for storing boats and RVs.

My routine as a single parent was established in a small unit on Narrabeen Beach. I modified business systems and organized staff to allow me the time to be with our children. I also spent time with one of my work colleagues, Fiona, whose love and affection were new and enlivening.

2000: Life after my divorce. Most of my old school friends had abandoned me (to put it kindly). Fiona and I spent six weeks traveling in Africa. Kindifarm continued to mature.

2001: Fiona and I were married on the Cocos Keeling Islands, a tiny island fifteen hundred miles off the west coast of Australia. With both Fiona and me working hard, Kindifarm boomed and was regarded as the industry leader.

2002: We bought a small beach house at Narrabeen so our kids could walk to the sand, play safely in a quiet street, and enjoy an outdoor lifestyle.

2003: Our daughter Brooke was born. I joined North Narrabeen Surf Club as a volunteer lifesaver. I started my fifth business, Dog Safety for Kids, after separating the sheepdogs from Kindifarm's menagerie.

Fiona and I spent many weekends driving out to the bush in search of buying her dream farm. We would walk the land and talk about what we could do with it.

2004: We found a property of interest and purchased a one-hundred-acre cattle farm, two-and-a-half hours north of Sydney. This was business number six, a cattle-breeding enterprise we affectionately call the Big Farm.

Decade Four Reflections

I now see that, during this decade, I was not strong enough to be honest with myself, and I ignored the signs of incompatibility with my first wife. I had fallen in love as a seventeen-year-old boy, traumatized by family loss but comforted by my girlfriend and the love of her family. Over the years, however, that comfort gave way to discomfort and felt false. The ignored truth became apparent. We lacked passion, true love, and intimate happiness. Our marriage was not fulfilling, and I didn't want to set that example for our kids.

Living the best life possible had become impossible. Eventually, I found the courage to face up to this reality, and in a split second of strength, I made the choice to divorce. This part of my journal helped me understand why I went back to that relationship each time over the years but finally listened to my *self* (that inner voice) and the man I wanted to be. I realized that being honest with myself—no matter what—was the most important principle I wanted to live by and that it takes time to uncover, process, and make peace within. Writing this journal gave me that time. It allowed me to forgive myself, the mother of our three beautiful children, and her family.

Falling in love again restored me, rescued me, and rejuvenated me. Fiona gave me the respect to stay true to myself. She understood my love of the land and the outdoors, and she shared my passion to live life the best we can. She also understood the importance of living a grounded life. Working with Fiona in business was both enjoyable and productive.

The time we spent looking for a farm should have immediately inspired me to return to the land, but now I could see that it often upset me, reminding me about what I had lost—those perfect golden years spent with Dad on beautiful cattle properties. I also kept so busy with Kindifarm that I didn't feel a burning desire to buy a real farm. After all, I had successfully created my own farm life in the city. Together, Fiona and I looked for property for well over a year, after which our financial situation improved, allowing us to look at better blocks of land that didn't require clearing and even cattle properties. That prospect of buying improved grazing land opened the emotional floodgates! All the years of struggling to adapt to life in the city erupted in a surge of passion and a reclamation of my country heritage. Now, I had reconnected with not only my love of the land but also the dream of a wife who loved the land.

Decade Five: 2005–2014

2005: I started waking at 5 AM to head over to the beach for a walk, listen to some self-help CDs, think, and have a swim. However, it never became a strong habit.

2006: I employed a business coach to help restructure Kindifarm like a franchise, with operations manuals and integrated systems, to improve the fast-growing business. During that coaching, I shared that I had been tinkering with creative writing for years and dreamed of making movies. I started to allocate time away from running the business to write an animated kids' television show called *Farm Tales*. I started jogging along Narrabeen Beach early in the morning a couple of times a week.

2007: After months of writing, I flew to Cannes, France, and New York City to pitch *Farm Tales* at two film and television production events. Finding what I believed to be interest in the project, I worked at taking the idea to the next level—a show that brings all my farm animals to the world. Kindifarm, meanwhile, was in trouble without my full attention and commitment. Given our debt situation (the mortgage on our home and a farm), young family, and overall busyness, I shelved the TV project.

2008: On my birthday, feeling overwhelmed with my busy life and still disappointed about the TV show, I had a moment of realization while holding a squealing piglet during a school event with Kindifarm. What was I doing? I rebooted my personal challenge to start a disciplined experiment of waking at 5 AM every weekday. My full commitment to these early hours fast-tracked many areas in my life, such as health, fitness, and happiness. Still overwhelmed by the business, I stepped up my experiment by starting work by 5:30 AM each morning to bring it under control. I was rewarded instantly, and all areas of the business improved greatly.

2009: I decided to document my early-rising experiment, with the sole purpose of giving myself an operational manual of sorts to live my own life by. I wrote my accidental life journal. I decided to sell Kindifarm.

2010: I successfully sold Kindifarm. I now had time to run the remaining smaller businesses and continue my 5 AM experiment and writing. I continued with the experiment of using the early mornings to write, go to the gym, swim in the surf, and most importantly, practice my developing self-improvement strategies.

2011–2013: I wrote most mornings, accumulating the first draft of a self-improvement book. I began coaching a small number of clients, calling the program the 5 AM Wake-Up Call.

2014: I sold Ponies for Parties and ceased operating Dog Safety for Kids. My old paid-by-the-hour business model was finally over. I earned more money with my more passive businesses (Kindifarm Horse Agistment and My Paddock Parking) than before the sale of the businesses and in a fraction of the time.

Decade Five Reflections

I cannot believe how busy my life had become! Although we tried to spend as much time on the farm as possible, business back in Sydney was extremely demanding. I was now essentially running six businesses, all requiring different demands. Fiona and I were burning out, and even though I had hired a business coach to help relieve some of the burdens and help me pursue my dream of working in film and television, it didn't work.

I felt like a failure. Kindifarm now represented all that was painful in my life. I felt trapped. I felt sick. I felt unhappy. This was rock bottom. I now understand that the failure with the TV show, *Farm Tales*, was one of the key lessons that motivated me to fully commit to and experiment with waking at 5 AM, develop self-improvement strategies, and write this book.

The most obvious outcome? I sold Kindifarm. I was then free to dedicate my newfound passion to my life's next adventure.

I was only able to do this after giving myself the time to reflect and empathize with the boy I had been and the man I had become. For the first time, after writing my accidental life journal, I had clarity around the events of my past and the external and internal forces that had been pushing me and pulling me toward an accidental life.

I could clearly see the conflict that had been raging within me for over forty years. And I now fully appreciated how much of an impact my first decade had on my life. I was my most authentic self when I was on the farm with Dad and when working the land as a jackaroo. I needed to honor that part of myself. This truth set me free.

LIVING AN INTENTIONAL LIFE

While your wake-up call may have arrived randomly—when your inner voice screamed out and you were ready to finally hear it—you now have a strategy to take back control and start living your life with intention. Completing your accidental life journal is an intentional act of self-examination to discover the truth about how and why you got here, who you are, where you want to go, and what you want to do. After you finish it, you will no longer be living an accidental life. It will be the line that you have drawn in the sand, behind which is your accidental life and in front of which is your new life, lived with intention. You will know your why. Living a life of intention will certainly include challenges—mine has. But the following chapters provide strategies that help you stay on course so you can continue living your best life.

CHAPTER 4

GOALS AND MAGNIFICENT OBSESSIONS

*What a different story men would have to tell if only
they would adopt a definite purpose, and stand by that until
it had time to become an all-consuming obsession!*

—Napoleon Hill, *Think and Grow Rich*

In the previous chapter, I tell you to write down your life's story until the present. You dig deep, you find your truth, you discover some forgotten dreams, and you make connections between your past and your present-day wake-up call.

The next pages in your life are up to you. How are they going to read? Are you going to get real and step up to your dreams? Or will you continue to wait for "someday," letting your fear and discouragement get in the way? In this chapter, you learn how to intentionally define your purpose, your dreams, goals, or perhaps your magnificent obsessions so you can live a new life of abundance.

WHY HAVING PURPOSE MATTERS

Reflecting on my accidental life journal helped me realize that I experienced exceptional growth during periods when I possessed a strong sense of purpose—jackarooing, tree planting, starting my business, redirecting my business, and buying a farm with my wife, to name a few.

Yet the truth is that some of these transformational episodes happened almost by coincidence. If you recall from the introduction of this book, I wouldn't have completed the Hay, Hell to Booligal Endurance Ride if I had not walked into that bar and seen the poster for it on the wall. In other words, the path I'd been following wasn't mapped out; it was random. Occasionally, my path intersected with underlying or even undiscovered goals—such as the endurance ride—that spoke to my true self. But how I found them was accidental.

So, what does this mean to the 5 AMer?

I mentioned earlier that the accidental nature of life is in many ways wonderful. However, we are exposed to many decisions and crossroads in life's direction every day, so a 5 AMer must decide which of those choices we act on with intention—not by accident.

A 5 AMer is intentional about waking up early to live life as best they can—a life of abundance. Therefore, as we progress each day, any option that presents itself can be assessed and decided on accordingly. Those that align with our intention can be acted on. Those that do not align can be discarded—it is always okay to say no and pass.

The important component is to always have the intention. That way, aligning your dreams, goals, and magnificent obsessions becomes easier, helping you live the best life possible. A life without intention gives you no reference, and so accidental encounters with opportunity are harder to recognize, are missed, or wrong decisions are made.

Your intention is your definite purpose—your why—that must become your all-consuming obsession. But before we talk about obsessions, let's talk about dreams because we all have them.

DREAMS, GOALS, AND MAGNIFICENT OBSESSIONS

I love dreams. We all love dreams. Dreams can take us away into a future of limitless possibilities. As a child, I dreamt of becoming a pilot. I still dream of owning a large farm. Dreams can make us feel good. They inspire us.

Dreams should be nurtured and allowed to run wild because they are the breeding grounds for goals. Napoleon Hill is believed to have said, "A goal is a dream with a deadline." I believe a deadline can also refer to the date and time we schedule to start working on a dream. Having an end date is a great benefit, but having a start date is exceedingly more important. Most dreams fail because they don't start—not because they don't cross the finish line.

There lies the difference that a 5 AMer must acknowledge. A dream will always remain a dream until it is acted on with intention. If you have a dream, you must activate it to become a goal, as set out in this book. Otherwise, it will never be realized, remaining a figment of your imagination or, worse, a regret reflected on in old age.

Throughout this book, I refer to goals many times because almost everything we act on is one, including the habit of waking early each morning to live a better life. We all dream of living a better life, but until we set the alarm (with the clear intention to improve ourselves), it remains a dream.

Waking up at 5 AM is your daily goal activation, which will become a hardwired habit, changing who you are in many ways. After successfully achieving that first goal of waking early, the entire day is a series of goal achievements—some very small and others large—but sure enough, goals all the same. More so, the advantage you gain when you activate those goals with discipline, persistence, focus, action, and passion, will more than likely result in success and the achievement of the life you desire.

Goal activation is outlined in detail shortly. However, the 5 AMer has an even greater advantage that almost guarantees the successful achievement of any activated goal no matter how crazy or out of reach it may seem.

That is the strategy of elevating a goal by making it a magnificent obsession.

A magnificent obsession is a goal that you mentally attached such a high level of importance, consequence, priority, value, attention, and gravity to, that it is mandatory—it is a "must do!" A magnificent obsession is compulsory. If you fail to achieve this goal, then you will feel incomplete, regretful, remorseful, resentful, defeated, and more. You must be willing to do almost anything to successfully achieve that goal.

Using the expression *magnificent obsession* is a strategy of mindset—
it emphasizes importance. To be magnificently obsessed with a goal, your
mindset must be dominated by the persistent idea of doing something
extraordinarily superb. When you attach that much importance to a goal, it
can make all the difference between success and failure.

The strategy of the 5 AM Advantage is that you can greatly benefit from
this evolution by deciding a dream now has a deadline to be activated as
a goal that (if required) can be elevated to magnificent obsession status,
whereby defeat is not an option.

That is the advantage that allows you to successfully achieve any dream
and any goal whether that's simply waking up earlier each day or redesigning
your entire life. As a 5 AMer, it's now a matter of making those decisions.

DO I HAVE A MAGNIFICENT OBSESSION?

As you write your accidental life journal, you (like me) may uncover a few
moments of inspiration and determination in your life—those moments or
events that you look back on with great pride and passion. This is a good place
to start because you begin to identify what weight of importance you have
given to various goals from your past. Success in your past may have come
from simply working hard toward achieving a goal or even from becoming
magnificently obsessed without realizing it. Now, understanding your own
success and defeats is how you activate future goals with intention.

But how do we know if a goal is simply a goal or if we need to become
magnificently obsessed and make it an all-consuming target that requires us
to hit the bull's-eye day after day? Most likely, year after year.

First, I like to think the goal is whatever the challenge or outcome is that
we decide to step up to, and the steps required to achieve that goal are simply
smaller goals. Like I write earlier, most of what we do each day is more or less
a series of goals—a series of steps.

Therefore, to successfully take each step, we must repetitively activate the goal at whatever level it takes to achieve success. However, certain
goals (because of their size, complexity, difficulty, and importance) may

additionally need to be elevated to magnificent obsession status. Otherwise, the likelihood of achievement may be greatly delayed, compromised, or even result in defeat.

Deciding on the size of a goal and when to elevate a goal to become a magnificent obsession will ultimately be determined by the individual and will, in many cases, change at different life stages. What once seemed so important may now not be a priority; it may even have become obsolete. A goal may evolve into a magnificent obsession, and one magnificent obsession may evolve into another. The evolutionary path is not equal to all. In chapter 1, I use the example of a runner who had a goal of running three miles on the beach but then achieved that goal and set sights on a marathon. This is a great example of how a goal can evolve into an obsession over time.

So how do you decide whether to become magnificently obsessed? One way is by stepping outside of your comfort zone. Part of what drives an accidental life is our inability to confront ourselves and our truths. It's easier to maintain the status quo—or adopt status quo goals even when they don't align with our true intention—because we don't have to question ourselves, risk being different, or risk failing. Remember, part of the reason I stayed with Kindifarm so long is that I looked successful to the people around me and they told me so; it was easy to believe it. It was more comfortable to simply continue—until it wasn't.

The problem, of course, is that stepping outside our comfort zone makes us uncomfortable, and we don't like being robbed of comfort. Because of this, becoming magnificently obsessed is rarely achieved. Sure, we can become sparked and excited, highly motivated and inspired to achieve a goal, but the required *obsession* often fails to materialize.

There are a couple of reasons for this. Our frantic and hurried pace of life is most often the culprit because it doesn't allow enough time, focus, or energy to transform our dreams into a mighty obsession—that's something waking up at 5 AM seeks to counter. But not knowing *what* to become obsessed with is equally the reason. After all, this decision is one of the most difficult we must face in life. Often, it takes time to find it. Your magnificent obsession may be buried by the lies we have told ourselves or others have told about us. It may be sunken under past failures or lost for years in a busy life full of commitments, distractions, dysfunctions, and responsibilities.

For the lucky few, the decision comes easy. Some even know before they finish high school, becoming high achievers at an early age. They're the lucky ones whose exploits and achievements we admire—Steven Spielberg, who wrote and directed his first film at sixteen, and Arnold Schwarzenegger, who envisioned becoming the youngest-ever Mr. Universe.

For most of us, however, our life's obsession is a mystery, a great unknown. Many of us wander through life, our mistakes and failures coloring our days and haunting our nights. We exist without purpose. How different our journey could be if we found our purpose—our why—and made it the torch that lights our path and devoted ourselves to reaching our full potential.

Is there something written out in your accidental life journal that is now haunting you? Did that process erupt a deep feeling of loss from a dream that has faded? Do you have an idea so wonderful, so desirable, so essential that if you fail to act on it your life will feel wasted?

I believe we all do. It may not feel as magnificent as becoming the world's most-bankable film director, but it is no less urgent or important in your own life. Do you hear an idea speaking to you, right now?

So ask yourself: *What is my magnificent obsession?*

To start, I suggest you decide that your intention to live a new life of abundance is your first magnificent obsession. This will be made up of many goals, one of which is to wake up early and activate all your goals throughout your day.

THE COST OF NOT BEING MAGNIFICENTLY OBSESSED

An accidental life journal clearly illustrates that we have many dreams and goals throughout our life. They may be achieved or not. They may be small or big, each requiring different levels of activation to achieve. Further, what is easily achievable for one person may be near impossible for another. But here's a warning: for some goals, especially those crazy ones that feel large and so out of reach, if it's not your magnificent obsession, its chance of success is greatly reduced.

How do I know? Writing my accidental life journal allowed me to finally see that one of my goals, to create a children's TV show, had not been elevated to a magnificent obsession. And it ended in defeat.

My story started in 2004, when I hired a business coach to help me systemize and restructure the operations of Kindifarm. My coach and I got along well and had great rapport as we shared many interests, such as horse riding. And even though I was meeting my business goals, she could tell I was unhappy and could sense my growing resentment toward that business.

My coach knew that I'd attended some screenwriting workshops in Sydney when I had returned from overseas. My unfinished scripts, notes, and ideas languished on the shelf in my home office. One day, we were having a casual conversation on the phone about those film scripts when she asked me, "When did you plan to include these creative ideas in your schedule?"

Is she kidding? I thought. Certainly, these dusty old outbursts of creativity weren't important enough to include in my current busy life! I let out a startled laugh and started to say she was actually right—I did *want* to act on those dreams *someday*. That's when my emotions clogged my throat, and I was cut off midsentence. Taken by surprise by my inability to answer, I broke down and began to cry uncontrollably. I closed my office door so my staff didn't hear me. I was literally speechless.

My coach's question had hit a raw nerve. My inner voice was screaming at me, longing to be heard. Because there was trust between my coach and me, I was able to be vulnerable. Now the truth was free. I was finally able to see things clearly. I had had the dream of writing a movie long before starting my business. I had put that dream on the back burner. In the quest to become "successful," I'd poured my energy into other responsibilities—work, family, kids, and a busy life.

Suddenly, I was desperate to change this even though I had hidden my dream and lied to myself about my passion for many years. I started questioning things: *Why had I done this to myself? Didn't I think I was good enough?*

Didn't I think my dreams deserved my passion, my energy? Why had I surrendered this dream? Why had I buried it? Why, why, why?

The answer was surprisingly simple. I was giving myself an out, an escape plan—an excuse. I had tricked myself into believing in Plan B with the reassurance that one day, sometime in the future, I might get to return to Plan A.

Someday.

I had not given my dream a deadline, and so it never became a goal. It had never even started, so it continued on over the years as a dream.

I had surrendered my entire life to Plan B. In fact, it seemed safer to live in Plan B, making sure my family's expectations were met, the bills paid, and my demanding job carried out each day while everyone else was happy and safe. Then, one day in the future, I would get to that bold, crazy, balls-out, selfish, and impossible Plan A. *It's okay*, I could think. *That's a relief! I haven't given up—nor am I unable, unwilling, lazy, cowardly, or full of shit for putting Plan A aside. I'm just doing the right thing, waiting for the right time for Plan A. I'm being a grown-up. I'm being responsible.*

Isn't that the story we often tell ourselves?

Isn't that how we all make it through the day, never coming to grips with the truth that we've crushed our spirits and buried our dreams?

Isn't that how we all get stuck, seeing that we're trapped by our lies but telling ourselves there's no way out?

I decided to change that. My business coach asked that I collate my ideas for screenplays, books, television shows, or any other creative ideas I'd had and carefully consider their merits before our next session. I decided on an animated children's TV series dreamt up from years of working with baby farm animals, observing their character and behavior, and seeing them interact with children. I'd long imagined creating a kid's cartoon show about a farm in a green valley where kids had discovered an ancient gift that allowed them to talk to animals. I called it *Farm Tales*.

I gave myself a deadline to start scheduling into my work week time away to develop my idea—that was my new goal. I learned that to pitch a TV show to a producer, I needed a series "bible" (an all-encompassing outline of everything in the show). So I developed all the characters, outlining their names, appearances, voices, and backstories. I outlined their needs, wants, personalities, specialties, fears, loves, favorite foods, and best friends. I commissioned an artist who drew all the characters, buildings, and imaginative landscapes that made up the show's world. I immersed myself and wrote thirteen episode premises, presented in a colorful forty-page bible that looked like it had been created by a team from a large production house, not some guy on a farm.

In 2006, nearly two years later, I flew to Cannes in France to attend an entertainment trade show called MIPCOM. Out of my comfort zone, I arrived with a bag of freshly printed *Farm Tales* bibles and business cards. Wearing my RM William boots (Australian cowboy boots) and a black Akubra hat (Australian cowboy hat), I prepared for sixteen meetings with TV executives from Europe, the United Kingdom, the United States, and India.

The atmosphere in Cannes was awe-inspiring—vibrant with gigantic posters of successful and upcoming shows hanging from the sides of posh hotels. The cafés were packed with people networking and looking important. On the second morning, I networked over eggs and coffee with other writers and creators. Previews were being shown in mini theatres for prospective buyers and production executives. That night, there were cocktail functions, dinners, and (for those wanting to party into the night) music.

For the next four days, I attended meetings, passionately outlining my vision for *Farm Tales*. Every meeting was pleasant and seemed to go well, yet I was filled with unease. I was out of my comfort zone—far away from my farm shed back in Australia—and couldn't tell if all the promises of future talks would actually come to pass. But I was working hard on my goal, so I was energized and felt proud to have stepped up.

When I returned home, I pushed on with a busy routine over many months, trying to balance my business work with pitching *Farm Tales*. Then, I flew overseas again, this time to New York to attend another television trade show, Kidscreen. Armed with the same kit, hat, and boots, I again stepped out of my comfort zone and into the world of show business. On the final day, I met with an American content buyer who seemed very interested in my project. His creative model included buying projects that he would joint-venture with other partners for production. This was exactly what I was looking for! After exchanging details, he promised to forward me a contract in the next few days.

The contract came through as promised—but to this day, I'm still not sure what happened. After reading the contract, I needed clarification on some of the details. I emailed a few questions I considered important. Days passed, but I never heard back. *Had I called the guy out on a bad deal with my questions? Maybe he'd simply changed his mind?* I'll never know. Over the following months, I continued taking meetings with local studios and production houses. But the momentum stalled, and I found myself without anyone interested enough to commit funding.

Meanwhile, although my Kindifarm management team had done an amazing job of dealing with my divided attention, I felt the business needed more of my energy and attention. My creative goal seemed futile anyway, so I set it aside once again, back on the "bookshelf." I was defeated.

THE GROWTH OF DEFEAT

I will always feel proud of what I did with *Farm Tales*, but the pain of failure runs deep. However, from all those years of working so hard toward defeat, I was rewarded with several of the most valuable lessons of my life.

Writing my accidental life journal and writing and researching for this book helped me see the truth. I had not fully committed to *Farm Tales* by making it my all-consuming magnificent obsession. I thought I had. After all, it wasn't like I just mildly attempted to make *Farm Tales* a reality. I had dedicated a couple of hard-working years to the project. I had placed enormous pressure on myself to step way out of my comfort zone—beyond what anyone else I knew was doing. By all my calculations, the payoff should have been huge!

But the truth is that I wasn't truly obsessed. Wow—that realization felt like a punch in the gut. But if I had made my goal mandatory, elevating it to magnificent obsession level, I wouldn't have given up. I would not have let work creep back in. I would have kept working on it as though my life depended on it. I would have given myself permission to stay with Plan A with the certainty of its success because that achievement was mandatory.

Once you have given a dream a deadline, you have a goal that will no doubt give rise to many smaller goals that serve as steps toward your final success. I now know that most goals can be successfully achieved when fully activated. However, some also need that extra advantage that results from the mindset of becoming magnificently obsessed. This can be critical for goals that rise from great ambition, but equally, to those that may seem small yet have been deemed mandatory (such as waking up early).

My goal of writing this book evolved into a magnificent obsession and as you continue over the following chapters, you will appreciate how it's taken me a lot more time and effort than I ever imagined. However, without such an elevated status that comes from being magnificently obsessed, I know with 100 percent certainty that it would have also ended in defeat.

Before we continue, please again reflect on your past. What was your mindset to those goals you achieved and those you failed to achieve? Did you fail to appreciate the importance of even the small goals? Did you fail to appreciate the bigger goals? Did you even see the goals? And did you fail to magnificently obsess over a goal that should have been made mandatory? Now is the time to see the patterns that guide each step you take as you live each day—goal by goal, day after day, year after year.

I also recognized that I had not correctly activated my goal of *Farm Tales*. These priceless lessons that resulted from many of my failings are detailed in the remaining chapters of this book. To successfully achieve any goal, from small challenges to those elevated to magnificent obsession status, the five goal activators—discipline, persistence, focus, action, and passion—give you the advantage to succeed, empowering you to change your life forever to live a new life of abundance.

CHAPTER 5

DISCIPLINE: THE FIRST GOAL ACTIVATOR

I t is said that when one applies the greatest effort possible to success-fully achieve something extraordinary, it takes blood, sweat, and tears. However, behind that struggle is a driving force that is so powerful that—when activated—almost anything you set your mind to is possible. It is a force that can be imposed on us; however, it is most commanding when it comes from within.

That force is discipline.

When we practice discipline, we have the self-mastery to climb methodi-cally, step by step, goal by goal, on the path to success. And in doing this, our thoughts are more certain, our actions are more productive, and our days are filled with purpose and gratitude.

Yet discipline is one of the most difficult concepts for many of us to embrace. You can have the greatest goal in the world or the smallest task to accomplish—yet, without discipline, you will not take each step necessary to achieve it.

The strategies outlined in this book can be difficult; there's no getting away from that fact. The more difficult something is, the more discipline it takes to stay the course. Without discipline, none of the other goal activators can succeed. In fact, without discipline, you won't even succeed in waking up at 5 AM each morning, let alone achieve your goals and magnificent obsessions.

For that reason, discipline is the first goal activator. I consider discipline the backbone of a 5 AMer, the thing that allows them to place one foot in front of the other, step by step until they reach their goal at last. In chapter 2, I define discipline as self-control. It's the ability to overcome the feelings, thoughts, weaknesses, and temptations that might otherwise steer you off course. Discipline is composure: you don't get rattled. Discipline is restraint: you don't act out. Discipline is the force of your will. And as the idiom goes, where there is a will, there's a way.

The good news? You get to practice discipline in its purest form every day by rising early. Discipline is like a muscle. If you exercise it, it becomes stronger. So every day that you wake up at 5 AM, your discipline muscle will grow stronger and stronger until, one day, any goal you take on is achievable. If you meet the challenge of continually waking at 5 AM, then you can meet the challenge of your goals. It also puts you in a disciplined mindset for the rest of the day. You already achieved one of the hardest parts of the day: you decided to overcome the temptation of staying in bed, with its warmth, comfort, and safety, even though you may have been sleepy, felt vulnerable, and wanted to go back to old habits of sleeping in. After overcoming all of that, what's stopping you from achieving whatever else you decide to do during the day? Discipline gives you the advantage.

Rising early tests your discipline at your first moment of consciousness. It demands a decision and results in the first action of your day. It's simple, and the results are easily measured—you either get up or you don't. You either achieve your goal or you don't.

MASTERING DISCIPLINE

Throughout the years when my alarm clock has awakened me at 5 AM, I reckon I have come up with most reasons *not* to wake up. Most of the year it is pitch dark with only the moon and stars still shining brightly. At best, there is predawn light. Often, it's cold and wet outside. It's warm and comfortable in bed. At times I've been unmotivated and have even questioned my obsession with early rising and my dogged mindset of always needing to step up to a challenge.

But as the years passed, fewer mornings resulted in the abandonment of my early rising plans. Now, I never fail to wake up and get out of bed when planned. This is because as each struggle to arise played out, I started to develop a set of rules that were tested, rewritten, and retested until I had mastered the discipline required in those early morning moments to always wake up.

THE TEN RULES FOR A DISCIPLINED 5 aMER

The following ten rules for a disciplined 5 AMer will help you become a master of early rising. This self-mastery is both the catalyst and an analogy for achieving so much more. Keep in mind that, like the five goal activators, these ten rules bleed together. They not only gain strength when used together but also rely heavily on each other to be effective and forceful.

Rule 1: Think It

Our mind is by far our strongest resource for mastering discipline (and everything else). That is why this rule—think it—heads the list. The first step to becoming a 5 AMer is thinking that you are a 5 AMer, even if you've never considered yourself a morning person. Practice believing that you have what it takes to rise early and achieve your dreams, and more likely than not, you will.

Becoming a 5 AMer all starts with an impulse, an initial thought that continues to play over in our mind until a decision is made. That process may be almost instantaneous, or it may take longer for you to reflect and weigh the pros and cons. But once you decide to become a 5 AMer, you must think as a 5 AMer—there is no sitting on the fence. When your mind is made up as to the person you must become and what you must do to get there, you gain clarity, become certain, and master waking at 5 AM. Furthermore, once your mind is made up that you're going to successfully achieve any goal, that goal is given life; it is activated. Success is now simply the process of doing what is required.

I can honestly say that being an early riser has changed my life like no other habit or strategy. That's why it's easy to focus my thoughts on the truth—I'm living life as best I can. The way we think about our lives and all the goals we face is extremely important. It's another thread in the cape we put over our shoulders that gives us superpowers.

I think like an early riser, not someone who struggles to wake. In fact, I mostly go to sleep at night with a real sense of excitement and adventure as to what the morning will deliver. After all, no morning is ever the same. Every sunrise is different. The rock pool I dive into will have changed from last time. One day, the still water is like a mirror, reflecting the orange colors from the horizon as the dawn breaks. Other times, the stormy waves crash over the pool, threatening to wash us over the sides and onto the rocks. It's exciting. It's uncertain. Even my gym workout changes with the varying schedule or the mood and conversation of my buddies. The first coffee of the day looking at the surf is always enjoyable.

Isn't this a better way to think about being an early riser than having conflicting thoughts that you're not a morning person or that you're just going to the gym, *again*?

The discipline to wake up early to work on a goal requires careful thinking. My goal to write this book was helped by thinking that I'm an author already. Becoming an author wasn't something I was going to do someday; it is who I am now. I'm not suggesting that we lie to ourselves—quite the opposite. We must be truthful in the language we use so it correctly reveals our legitimacy. The definition of *author* is a writer of a book, article, or document. There's nothing in the definition that says an author must write a certain number of words or be published to earn the title. Therefore, if I sit down to write this manuscript, I am an author. I am legitimate. When I was waking up in the dark of winter to write, this way of thinking helped me become disciplined to head to the keyboard instead of hitting snooze. I would often think, *This is what an author must do when writing a book.* And so I did it.

PRACTICE THINKING IT

Before you go to sleep, think about the person you must become and what goal you are achieving. More so, be truthful in your thinking. In many ways, you are already that person. The next morning when the alarm clock goes off, think it: *I am [what you want to be], and I am [what you want to achieve].* For me, it might be, "I am an author, and I am writing a book." This is the split second to be totally honest and think deeply about who you are becoming and the goal you are achieving by placing your feet on the floor. Think of nothing else. Think it, and step up.

Rule 2: Own It

There is only one person who can make the habit of early rising an enjoyable and essential part of your life. There is only one person who can make the habit something you cannot possibly go without, one that makes you feel you are succeeding with your goal each waking morning.

That person is you. You must own it. And you must own the outcome of your day because there is simply no one else you can blame.

When writing my accidental life journal, I remembered a valuable lesson I learned during the summer I planted pine trees in the wilderness of British Columbia, Canada. Thousands of acres of mountainous land had been cleared by logging companies, and it all had to be replanted by hand with new pine tree seedlings. This was extremely hard work. I spent each day—sunrise to sunset, seven days a week—clambering over the cleared landscape with a backpack full of small trees. Each morning around 5 AM, the supervisor would walk around the camp, playing heavy metal music on a boom box to wake everyone up. I didn't want to get up. No one wanted to get up. It was dark, very cold, way too early, and we were exhausted, knowing more hard work awaited as we battled mind and body.

During those times, I absolutely hated getting up. But I did, day after day. The heavy metal music would infiltrate my dreams, getting louder and louder until it was outside my VW Kombi, waking me up. The realization that the music was not in my dream, it was an alarm clock, was always shocking. But I dragged myself out of bed without fail because I was determined to make this an experience of a lifetime. I had fully committed to completing the contract and owned every minute of it.

This is easier to write about now than it was to do. At that time, the skin on my hands had dried out so much from planting the seedlings that they had cracked to the point of bleeding. I wrapped my fingers in duct tape to keep them from opening right up. At times, the insects were so thick in the air that it was impossible not to breathe them in, and I was always badly bitten. The weeks without showering pushed us all to the edge of becoming totally feral, but still, I owned every second. I may not have liked it at that moment, but I knew succeeding in the challenge I had set for myself was worth the effort. I would overcome adversity. I owned it. When others quit, I pushed on. After the contract was completed, I was offered another. Which I accepted.

Owning it is a powerful and highly productive rule for the 5 AMer as you work toward achieving any goal, especially when it's hard, you don't like it, or even if it seems to be something out of your control.

The 5 AM Advantage makes us responsible for the small action of waking up. The discipline we practice every day when we wake up enables us to also take responsibility for all the other actions we take or don't take in life. It's up to us, and only us.

This is also true when life throws us curveballs. We may not be able to control everything that happens to us—and some events, such as my accident with the bull, will result in traumatic and life-changing consequences—but we can still own how we react to those consequences. We are, therefore, ultimately responsible for how every experience colors our lives during good times and bad, whether chosen or not.

Often, owning our actions makes us uneasy. We pivot back and forth in a state of stagnation and indecision: yes, no, yes, no, yes. Yet, in the end, it comes down to a split-second decision. In an instant, we choose to jump off the cliff with a leap of faith. We step up. We own it. This is the moment we face each morning when the 5 AM alarm goes off.

> ## PRACTICE OWNING IT
>
> Each morning when your alarm goes off, ask yourself the following question: "Am I too tired to wake up?" Then properly own the question by asking the real question: "Am I too tired to wake up to successfully work toward my goal?" This answer holds you accountable to the outcome, which is succeeding or failing to achieve your goal. The truth is that the answer is no. Own it and wake up.

Rule 3: Know Your Why

Rules 1 and 2 are empowered by rule 3: know your why. Your why is your extraordinary reason for waking up to work toward achieving your goal each morning. Your why is the fuel you throw on the fire so that your goal explodes into a passionate rage, a life quest, a battle, or a magnificent obsession. Your why is the most powerful resource you have now, or will ever have, to help you wake up and then step up to any challenge—no matter how small or large that may be. You must awake to your why.

Why did I push through the weeks of pain in the wilderness of British Columbia? Because I needed to prove to myself and all the others I was working with that I was capable. I needed to prove to myself that I was worthy. That I was strong. That I could be relied on. Trusted to complete a challenge. That I was a man.

Your why is personal. If it's not, then make it personal. No one else needs to ever know your why. Load up as many whys as you can. Dig deep. Make them emotional. Get your blood pumping and the tears flowing!

Why did I ride across the desert on my horse Blue Boy? Because my dad was an expert horseman and I wasn't. Because I knew this race would force me to step up and become the horse rider I wanted to be. Because I loved a challenge. I wanted to push myself. I wanted to know that I could do it. I wanted to respect myself. I wanted to love myself. I needed to prove it.

Why have I woken up at 5 AM for nearly two decades? Because I want to live every day to the fullest, and having an early start helps me feel I am. I feel shame for those mornings I slept in as a young man with a hangover, waking up feeling like shit. I don't want to waste another morning again. After all, none of us know what's coming. I might be running out of time. I have so much more to do in life, and I want to live life better. I don't want to let down my buddies in the morning. I love seeing the sunrise. I love going to bed tired, ready for sleep, and exhausted, knowing I fully lived the day.

As you can see, my whys are personal, and they may have little or no effect on you. But the point is that my whys have had a massive influence on me. They have been explosive. You need to find the same in your own why.

Digging deep to find your why is when the magic happens. Every morning you have a golden opportunity to give yourself an audacious why. If you limit your why, you limit your likelihood of success. If you limit your why, you limit how significant and life-changing your goal can be. Your why must be so influential to your thinking that it annihilates any resistance you may come up against. Your why must be so personal and emotional that you own it more than anyone else in the world. Your why must be so big that it smashes any negativity, sabotage, or competition from those who may attempt to derail your goal.

FIND YOUR WHY

Time to dig deep. Time to be honest. Time to be vulnerable. Throughout your day, allow yourself the time to start understanding the reason behind your quest by simply asking, "What is my why?" Be specific. Make it personal. Why are you waking up at 5 AM tomorrow morning? Why is the goal you are working toward so important? This may require more reflection from your accidental life journal.

Additionally, who must you do this for? After all, we would give our life for the safety of someone we love in a heartbeat, so now ask yourself—whom will you dedicate this quest to? They are your why.

Rule 4: Create a Framework

To develop the discipline of being a 5 AMer, you must know what rules you are playing by, otherwise your intentions become uncertain. That's why this rule is about creating a framework. A framework is the basic structure, plan, or set of rules a 5 AMer decides to live or work by. It tells you what you're going to do each morning, providing clarity and certainty and removing confusion from the equation.

For example, perhaps you decide to wake up at 5 AM five mornings a week to improve personal fitness before going to work. You know exactly what you are going to do each morning: wake up, exercise, improve your fitness. It's straightforward.

Without a plan—or with only a vague plan—there is no way to tell if you're on track to achieve your goal. Someone who intends to wake up early to vaguely work on a goal will quickly become confused about or unsure of whether they are doing what they need to do. If your goal is to improve fitness, but you have not specified what you're going to do or when you're going to do it, then it's easy to get lost or sidetracked. Without the certainty of what action you need to take when the alarm goes off in the morning—if it was set at all—it will be easier for conflicting thoughts to prevail, and you may start questioning yourself: Do I really need to wake up early today? Maybe it's okay to start tomorrow.

When you have a framework that outlines the actions you need to take to achieve your goal, it's much easier to fend off negative questions. Do I really need to wake up early today? Yes, I must exercise today to energize myself and make my body stronger.

This example, while simple, will work if it's rigorously adhered to. Therefore, when the framework has been set, it must be followed. This is how you strengthen discipline. This is how goals are successfully achieved.

Although your framework can outline your plan broadly, you can make it as specific as you wish. To refine the previous example, you could outline the exact days of the week you will exercise, what exercise you will do, and for how long. It's not always necessary, but you can drill down as deep as you'd like to flesh out details. It will still work as long as you follow the plan.

Your framework will change over time. Goals are achieved, new goals are set, we get older, and the years pass, giving us a new and fresh perspective on what is important and what we must work toward. The evolution of the framework synchronizes with the evolution of our lives; this is how we grow and live better.

But the time to change the framework is never at 5 AM. That is not the time to reconsider and reassess your plan, as your thoughts may be blinded to your real goals. After all, it's cold and dark outside, and the bed is warm and comfortable—who *wouldn't* question the move from comfort to discomfort? Instead, update your framework during the day or in the evening before the alarm is set. This is when your thoughts will be in line with your goals.

I have decided on many frameworks over the years. One framework had me swimming in the local ocean rock pool six mornings a week. I was up at 5 AM and into the pool by 5:25 AM. I know this because the pool lights come on at 5:30 AM, usually halfway through my third lap. That was after my accident with the bull, when I needed to focus on getting my health back. For four years straight, the framework focused on nothing but my early morning rehabilitation and recovery.

Before that, however, my framework set out a plan to be up at 5 AM Monday, Wednesday, and Friday mornings, sitting at my home office desk by 5:15 AM to write an earlier draft of this book. On Tuesday and Thursday mornings, I was scheduled to be at the surf club, working out in the gym, and then having a swim, followed by a coffee with my surf club patrol. On Saturday morning, I swam in the rock pool and then had a casual weekend breakfast with the same surf club buddies. Sundays, I slept in. Every week, the same routine. Today, the details of my framework are a little different, but its general structure remains constant, framing up the long-term view of how I choose to live my life.

CREATE A FRAMEWORK

Open your laptop or favorite notebook because now is the time to start physically creating your framework by answering the following questions. What is your routine? What time are you going to wake up? How many mornings are you going to wake up early? What are you going to do with those mornings? Remember, you can always update your framework. It may be better to establish just a few mornings of early rising or even start at 5:30 AM and use the momentum of that success to raise the bar. You're in this for the long term, so be strategic and have patience. Your evolution takes time.

Additionally, what advice can you seek to help set your framework—a personal trainer, a life coach, your peers, or a business advisor? It will always help to use a proven framework, so take some time to research and copy any that align with your goals.

Rule 5: Be Prepared

When you are not properly prepared for the challenge ahead, you will sabotage your goals with doubtful thoughts and derail them through disorganized practice. When you are prepared, you sharpen the certainty you gained from having a framework and you increase your control over your practice.

A large chunk of your goal is achieved in your preparation for it. I like to think that when I'm prepared, I'm already halfway there. With this mindset, waking up at 5 AM to work on the second half of the goal is relatively easy.

Part of your preparation means physically organizing everything you need to productively work on your goal in the morning. For example, on days when I'm scheduled to write, I tidy my home office desk so I'm ready to work without delay, I'll have a drink bottle filled, and I make sure the coffee is ground and loaded for brewing in the morning. On days that I'm scheduled to work out, I lay out my shorts, shirt, sweat top, shoes, and socks on the floor. I put the key to the surf club door next to my clothes. I pack my gym bag with a beach towel, change of clothes, Crossover Symmetry bands, a water bottle, and a small coin pouch with exactly $4.50 to pay for my coffee.

If any of these preparations fail, I may have to look for clothes in the dark, which may wake up my wife (very unfair). Or I would waste time and energy, making me late to the gym. Once there, I may be without an important item that allows me to successfully achieve my morning goals. Maybe a forgotten beach towel—not good in the cold of winter. Anything that goes wrong can make it easier to give up.

Being prepared also means being mentally prepared. Mentally prepare for the morning each evening by taking a few moments to think it (whom do I want to become?), own it (this is up to me and no one else), and know why (I must do this so I can show my family I'm up to the challenge of making our lives amazing). The better prepared you are for this thought pattern, the better you will react when it's *go time*. Instead of the alarm startling you awake, you will expect it. It's like expecting the firing gun at the start of a race, so you won't stumble out of the block, you'll be off and running.

Remember, even small goals can be derailed through a lack of preparation. This is completely preventable through proper groundwork. Be prepared, and you're halfway there.

PRACTICE BEING PREPARED

What do you need to do today so the goal you will be working on in the morning is best set up for you to achieve it? Make a list or run through your morning routine in your mind to see everything you will need, and lay it all out and have it ready, so your morning energy flows without a hitch.

What thought process is going to help you spring out of bed when that alarm goes off at 5 AM? How can you get prepared tonight before you go to sleep so that your thought process is a powerful driving force? Try reading a short, prepared note you leave next to your bed outlining the person you want to become, emphasizing that you own it, and exaggerating your why. Repeat this until a paper note is no longer required and it's an automatic nightly affirmation.

When you reach to turn the light off, feel excited that tomorrow you're waking up to work toward those goals that you know are making you a better person.

Rule 6: Make a Decision

Making decisions can be one of the hardest things we do in life, but no matter how long it takes to arrive at one, when it comes, it happens in a split second. Our day, and therefore our life, is made up of a series of decisions.

The 5 AM Advantage allows us to exercise the discipline required to make good decisions from the beginning of each day, right when the alarm clock goes off. In fact, I refer to the alarm clock as a "decision alarm," because in the split second it goes off, you are faced with your first decision of the day: Do I wake up?

No, the alarm clock is not just a daily nuisance that goes off loudly and abruptly to jolt you out of bed. It represents decision time.

The advantage for the 5 AMer is threefold. First, when we acknowledge the alarm clock represents the first decision of the day, then we know that many other goal-related decisions will soon follow, making us pay attention. In other words, those decisions become clearer as they come into focus. We develop the discipline to see them and step up to them instead of letting them pass us by. We are active instead of inactive or reactive. We stay in control—decision after decision and day after day.

Second, when we are aware of decision time, no matter when it occurs in the day, we can evaluate how a decision will move us toward our goal (or not). We can weigh its importance and urgency, look at options, and seek advice or upskill to then make a better decision.

Third, when we are aware of the decision and how it was made, we can measure how well we made the decision. Did you make a good decision or a bad one? Did you wake up to work hard on the next step that will move you closer to success, or did you hit the snooze button and stagnate? Now that the decision's worth has been measured, you can use the ten rules to adjust your approach before making the next decision. This will allow you to progress, advancing goal achievement and improving your life in general.

My accidental life journal revealed how making decisions on the run, not giving them due thought, and ignoring them resulted in lost time and direction, regret, unhappiness, and so on. Now that I think like a 5 AMer, I see the crossroads where decisions need to be made, and I know that even the small decisions matter. For example, I have a decision to make as I type: Do I keep writing or stop and go to the beach? It's a beautiful summer day and the beach would be great. But if I'm going to meet my deadline, finishing this section now is the right decision. Also, I had a swim at sunrise as part of my daily framework. I built something important to me—the beach—into my exercise routine, so I never miss out. This makes the decision (in this case, writing) an easier one to make.

My decision to keep writing may appear so simple, you could easily dismiss its relevance. But simplicity is powerful. We overlook many small, simple decisions that help us work effectively on our goals, especially when we move through the day on autopilot. Those simple decisions add up. Later, we're left wondering why achieving goals is so hard. Successfully achieving those goals requires discipline—part of which is thoughtfully making decision after decision, no matter how small—to keep you on track. Discipline prevents you from wasting time.

Paul, one of my coaching clients, shared his experience with his decision alarm. "I had a million different alarm clocks," he told me. "Some on my desk away from bed, even one on wheels that runs away from you. But in my sleepy stupor, I'd always quickly get up, press the button, and then go back to bed. I have my new alarm clock with a disarm panel at the other end of the house, which has somewhat improved my situation. However, I sometimes wake up and convince myself that I need more sleep and disarm it. Then, when I finally wake up with clarity, I think, *Why did I do that?*"

Paul's honest revelation underscores that the alarm clock truly represents decision time and that we can easily assess whether we've made a good or bad one. This empowers us to have clearer and more precise thoughts at that waking moment. *Okay, the alarm has gone off. Now, it's time to decide—do I wake up?* Furthermore, as we become aware of this thought pattern, a 5 AMer improves on hearing other questions throughout the day.

Understanding that our day is a series of decisions should not, however, trap us into a never-ending cycle of worrying over the consequences. For sure, some decisions have major consequences and need to be well thought through, but many are not so critical. In chapter 7, you learn how to focus decisions with mind mapping to remove overload. But for now, keep in mind that it takes mistakes to learn, adjust, and improve. You're free to blunder, step out of your comfort zone, take risks, or simply make decisions faster.

An alarm is an essential tool for the 5 AMer—however, a blaring alarm clock is not the holy grail for waking early. Choose whatever device, even if it's quiet, that will help alert you to your first decision of the day. I personally use my iPhone Bedtime clock so I can have its volume set on low. It also allows me to decide which days of the week it goes off, and it has a good selection of decision alarm sounds. That way, when it goes off Monday through Friday at 5:00 AM and Saturdays at 5:15 AM, a very quiet, peaceful melody starts up without waking my wife. It also shows how many hours of sleep I plan to get, which I can check against my framework.

At the end of the day—or should I say the start of the day—it's not about the alarm clock itself. It's about *what* you choose to do in that split second after the decision alarm goes off. Make your decision wisely.

PRACTICE MAKING A DECISION

As a constant reminder to yourself that it's time to make a decision, customize the title on your phone's alarm or put a sticky note on or next to your alarm clock, saying, "decision alarm!" so it's the first thing you see each morning.

Be certain about what decision you will need to make when the decision alarm goes off. Reinforce your why and own it. There is literally only

continued →

one person in the world who, at that split second, needs to make the decision—you! Then try putting a sticky note on your bathroom mirror saying, "decision time," so that when you step up from bed and head to the bathroom, you are reminded that it's time to make the next decision about what action *must* be taken in the next sixty minutes.

What other tools can you use from the ten rules of discipline that will help make that decision? Arm the decision with as many tools as you can to the point that making the decision becomes easy and automatic.

What other decisions do you expect tomorrow as you work on your goal? What seemingly unimportant decisions might you need to be aware of tomorrow? How are you going to decide?

How can you empower moments when decisions arise, no matter how small or large, so they too become easy and automatic?

Where else can you stick "decision time" sticky notes? Maybe on your gym bag or office desk? Add a few keywords to the note to trigger your why, your ownership—whatever helps you make the right decision.

Rule 7: Apply Pleasure or Pain

It's natural to fantasize about the benefits that will result from taking action toward the achievement of your goals. Similarly, it's natural to dwell on pain and discomfort when those goals are ignored, deprioritized, and put on the "someday" list in a busy life.

Having a 5 AM mindset, however, means you can focus, exaggerate, and overemphasize those feelings so the pleasure or pain can be harnessed and used as a voice of encouragement throughout the day—especially at the moment the decision alarm goes off.

To harness the motivating power of pleasure, every thought, word, or action associated with waking at 5 AM and the goals you're working toward must anchor you to positivity, high energy, and complete certainty that your goals are both achievable and underway. For example, when you're thinking about waking in the morning, do so with intense focus on how great you will feel when you succeed. Positive thinking can feel good because it releases feel-good chemicals in the brain. These chemicals, such as dopamine and serotonin, can improve mood, reduce stress and anxiety, and increase overall well-being. Additionally, a focus on pleasurable emotions can shift our perspective and make us feel more optimistic, hopeful, and motivated, leading to better problem-solving and decision-making. After all, being in control of your life and living it to the maximum feels incredible—and your body and mind know it.

Sharing your goals with others is important, but the most important conversation you have is with yourself! Positive self-talk is fundamental to this rule. You can boost positive thinking by focusing on body movements as well. Be aware of your body's posture and facial expression. For example, when you stand with confidence—tall, with your head slightly lifted, chest slightly extended, and with a look of determination—you increase your certainty that you will achieve your goals, increasing pleasure. If you stand defeated—stooping with a frown on your face—you will feel weaker and vulnerable to failure, increasing pain.

Develop the habit of checking and adjusting your posture and facial expression before making a decision. For example, when your decision alarm goes off, smile as you think about waking, putting on your shoes, and jogging out into the darkness. This will anchor those thoughts to pleasure. You might even clench your fist and say, "Yes!" at the thought of hearing your feet hit the pavement, sitting down to write your novel, or getting that million-dollar deal over the line. Tony Robbins refers to this simple and powerful gesture as your *power move*. Feel the pleasure of the person you are becoming. Experience the power of who you are right now. Apply the pleasure and amplify it.

On the flip side, if you didn't manage to wake up on time, apply pain by giving yourself negative feedback using the same intensely focused thoughts to feel mental and emotional anguish. This may sound harsh, but if your framework directs you to rise at 5 AM and you throw the decision alarm across the room and sleep in until 7 AM, you need to correct yourself! Ask yourself this: If I can't succeed at the simple challenge of waking early, how the hell am I going to achieve my bigger goal? So toughen up, buttercup—or all your friends and family will know you're a loser, and you'll be doing the same old shit for the rest of your life.

I think you get the message. (Ouch, language hurts!) Use it to your advantage. Your internal dialogue is no doubt the biggest influence on your life. So the reality is that if you fail to wake up on time or fail to work on your dream, the conversation you have with yourself is going to be that of disappointment, disgust, anguish, and pain anyway. You can harness that! Turn negative thoughts into intentional internal dialogue that will help you make a better decision next time. After the pain has been delivered, stop. We're not trying to punish ourselves. We're applying a short, sharp jolt to inspire change, knowing both pleasure and pain are critical components of your mindset. One is powerless without the other. Together, both are incredible tools for transformation.

Applying pleasure and pain can be used in an instant to strengthen discipline and achieve a goal. To effectively use them, you must make a direct contrast between where you will be in the future if you don't achieve the goal and where you'll be if you do. With a moment or two of deep thought, focus on how much of a struggle life will it be if you keep doing what you're doing and procrastinate. What will life be like if you never achieve that dream? What is the cost of stagnation? Allow yourself to feel the pain of failure. Feel the deep dissatisfaction within your gut if you continue to stagnate. Cry out in pain and tell yourself off with a look of defeat. Feel it and live it. Do this for as long as it takes to move you to the core.

Feel it so intensely that you actually feel like you've lost it all. Then go to the other extreme. What will your life look like if you wake up early each morning and work persistently toward your dream? Really picture living this dream! How do you feel? How healthy are you? Where are you living? Who is in your life? You are living the dream; you're a success! Stand tall, shoulders back, and legs slightly apart and strongly anchored. Now, do a fist pump or simply squeeze your hand, shout out, and take it to the next level.

Imagine if everything you dreamed of was your reality. Everything. Feel the pleasure. Say, "Yes!" and you will be compelled to take action. Massive action!

The morning conversation you have with yourself is critical. Some mornings, your inner dialogue will be the voice of incredible pleasure; other mornings, it will be screaming at you from a place of failure and pain. After all these years, I still have mornings when I hesitate to jump out of bed. On those mornings, I think it, own it, and know my why. I have a clear framework, I'm well prepared, and I know it's decision time. So I immediately go through the pain and pleasure scenarios. It's all part of the strategy—and it's essential that you practice it every morning when needed. Continue to practice. You must become your own personal motivational speaker, life coach, and most avid #1 fan. Repeat to yourself how fantastic it is that you are working toward your goals! Cheer yourself on, bet on yourself, and arouse all the positive feelings about what you're doing and all the obstacles you're overcoming. Shout out in your thoughts, "I am finally on the way to achieving my dream. It's really happening!"

PRACTICE APPLYING PLEASURE AND PAIN

To strengthen discipline when the decision alarm goes off, associate an immediate and massive burst of pleasure with the decision you are making to wake up. I'm talking about giving yourself a jolt of pleasure, something that will bounce you out of bed. In fact, you may end up leaping out of bed before the decision alarm goes off. "I'm ready to take on the world!" you'll cry out, your fists pumping and chest extended. Take time to answer the following questions: What are your triggers for pleasure and pain? Know your why and exaggerate the consequences. What will you gain with success? What will you lose with failure? What is at risk? Dig deep and truly feel how these emotions move you.

Rule 8: Reward Yourself

A reward is that famous "carrot" that is used to move the horse that pulls the cart. Physical rewards provoke or act as a trigger for pleasure. Rewarding yourself can amplify the positive and negative self-talk of rule 7, motivating you to stay steadfast.

Just like positive self-talk, a reward can activate the release of dopamine, which motivates us to seek rewards in the future. In other words, the potential for pleasure can influence your mindset and behavior, leading you to repeat the thinking and acting that led to reward. This creates a positive feedback loop, and this is what helps you resist temptations, overcome obstacles, and stay on the path toward your goal.

While rewards offered to us are effective, the best rewards are the ones we set ourselves, as they can be customized to suit our individual needs and desires. If you want to have the discipline to bounce out of bed at 5 AM, set your framework to include rewards when you succeed. Perhaps, if you wake up as planned for a certain given period—say one week—you buy or do something special. Whatever the reward is, decide right now and put a sticky note on your computer screen or fridge. *Right now.* This is the reward that will result from you taking a defined action. And don't be stingy with the reward—make it worthwhile.

Moving forward, set yourself certain milestones and decide on the subsequent rewards. What's a good reward if you wake up at 5 AM to work on your goal for an entire month? Or when certain goals are achieved? After my first three months of waking at 5 AM, I rewarded myself with a new, custom-made surfboard. I still remember the pleasure I felt as I ran my hands over the fiberglass, feeling the rails and the smooth finish of the board—truly a beautiful thing to hold (if you're a surfer, you'll understand what I mean)—before heading out for my first surf.

Obviously, we can't reward ourselves like this for everything we do, as the benefits would quickly diminish—and we might go broke. But this is an essential strategy for those challenges we find difficult. Especially when you're new to early rising. However, over the years, I have used this rule in many ways. For example, delayed gratification can be highly rewarding. You can achieve this by delaying an ordinary activity that you already enjoy. For example, maybe you will not let yourself have your morning cup of coffee until you work a certain number of minutes on your business plan.

Whatever it is, when you finally reward yourself, your body will release those feel-good chemicals and your daily pleasure will feel even more like a treat, giving you the motivation you need to stay on track. Sometimes, the simplest rewards can make all the difference in successfully achieving a goal.

I took delayed gratification to the next level with some of my big goals. I call this strategy *reward conversion*. At one point, I needed to buy a new SUV, as my Landcruiser had traveled over 250,000 miles, so I decided to convert that purchase into one mighty big reward. Unless my current Landcruiser blew up earlier, I decided that there was no way on earth I would purchase the new vehicle *before* my book draft was completed—and that required me to stay firm on my goal.

I also developed a strategy called *reward stacking*. If one reward can provide the motivation to stay on track, why not ramp up the benefits with multiple incentives? For example, I wanted to buy a drone to shoot great footage for my coaching videos. I decided to stack this reward with the new SUV. I wouldn't purchase either unless I finished my book draft.

Converting and stacking rewards prevents you from straying from your goal and increases motivation because the reward is now bigger. This can help you achieve that goal faster. Oh, and it's fun! There's no limit to how many rewards you stack, and the more creative you are, the better. After all, it's an investment into your own success.

All the rewards I have described so far are extrinsic—they are physical, coming from external sources. But there's a second type of reward, an intrinsic reward. These are rewards that come from within, such as a sense of accomplishment or satisfaction.

The motivation gained from extrinsic rewards may peter out in the long run. Intrinsic rewards tend to last longer. Gregory Careman, author and founder of the Brain Academy, suggests that *extrinsic* rewards that are solely based on results (such as the surfboard) face this problem—if the result is not achieved and the reward not given, you risk giving up because the pleasure was never experienced.[5] *Intrinsic* rewards, however, are directly linked to a

5 Gregory Careman, *Neuroplasticity: How to Rewire the Brain*, section 3, part 14, "Starting New Habits," accessed September 13, 2023, https://www.brainacademy.com/p/neuroplasticity2-0.

behavior, not a result. So the new habit of waking up at 5 AM to work on a specific goal, for example, brings joy by simply doing it.

My personal experience aligns with this. I receive joy from going to the gym and working out with my surf club mates before the sun rises. I receive joy from writing on a cold morning in the dark beside a log fire at the farm. I receive joy during the act, not just when it's completed. Over the years, I have realized that the rewards that come from within are the ultimate reward. Happiness, self-love, pride, worthiness—these rewards are priceless.

PRACTICE REWARDING YOURSELF

You must gain clarity and have a strong emotional association with your *carrot*, so the rewards when you successfully achieve your goals are anticipated with enthusiasm. Ask yourself: What small reward will motivate you to wake up tomorrow at 5 AM? What massive reward will motivate you to work on a goal like your life depends on it? What milestones can you set, and what rewards can you put on offer? Is there something you want anyway that you can convert into a reward? What rewards can you stack up together? How can you nurture gratitude to receive the best rewards, those that come from within?

Rule 9: Be Flexible and Reject Perfection

By now, you should understand that discipline is our ability to control our thoughts, actions, and impulses to achieve a goal. It involves setting clear a framework, developing a plan, and following through until success is achieved. While discipline can help you achieve high standards and excellence, it does not require perfection.

The problem with perfection is that it is unattainable and leads to feelings of failure and dissatisfaction. Additionally, striving for perfection leads to excessive stress and a lack of balance in life, and it discourages us from taking risks, being creative, and trying new things. Perfection cuts us down, branding us a failure. Therefore, perfection is not only unrealistic but also the enemy.

Flexibility, on the other hand, allows us to adapt to changes and unexpected challenges and to learn from our mistakes. It allows us to maintain a sense of accomplishment and continue to progress along the path of success, which may be long. Flexibility empowers us with a mindset of success. Therefore, flexibility is our friend. It is the only way to successfully achieve our goals.

As you know, I have been waking up at 5 AM for about eighteen years. However, if I was unrealistically striving for perfection, I could not make this claim. There have been periods—such as while I was recovering from the bull accident—when I did not wake up at 5 AM every day. When measured against perfection, this makes me a failure. But by building flexibility into my mindset, I am a success. I understand that emergencies are going to crop up and affect my routine, and if I give myself grace when I need it and get back to my routine when I am able, that is all I can expect of myself. After all, no one is perfect.

Because perfection is unattainable, there will always be more to do. Personally, I could have written my book faster, I could still be fitter, my new business could be better, I could be happier, I could be wealthier, and so on. But when we take perfection as the goal, we will always see that we have fallen short instead of recognizing how far we've come.

Perfection is a destructive, distorted vision. It is impossible to live a perfect life. Full stop.

The earlier rules show us that through our so-called failings, we can rally the strength to climb out of the depths of defeat. In fact, sometimes it's necessary for us to feel the pain of defeat to harness the resulting energy and grit to ultimately get the job done. In this way, we overcome unimaginable obstacles and hardships. But that's not the same thing as expecting perfection from ourselves.

As a 5 AMer, there are many reasons to add flexibility to your framework from the outset. Work demands, physical and mental health issues, social events, weekends, and holidays are all part of a balanced life. A balanced life gives you the energy to keep going. The quest for perfection will quickly wear you down.

For example, when I'm on holiday in a new country, I may decide to wake up at 5 AM to experience dawn from a new culture and perspective. Or I may not. When a friend from out of town drops over for dinner and we stay up late, even a bit too late, I may decide to turn my alarm clock off before I go to bed. Or I may not. Flexibility helps avoid burnout.

At no time during those occasions when flexibility was appropriate did I throw the routine of early rising away. It was temporary. Flexibility is a critical component of the 5 AM Advantage, giving it the ultimate strength to succeed over the long term. And, as you read in the next chapter, it always takes a long-term view to succeed in our goals. A mighty tree doesn't stand for thousands of years by being stiff. It stands by bending to the wind. By being flexible.

There is one caveat to this rule: you must be honest with yourself about how flexible you are being. Flexibility may be our friend, but it is not an opening to back down from a challenge, let yourself off the hook, or rescind an agreement with yourself. It must not be abused. If we begin to be too flexible, we must call ourselves out.

It's one thing to stay up late with an out-of-town friend whom you rarely see and who isn't in town long. Without flexibility, you'd be missing out on an important opportunity to maintain that friendship. It's another thing to stay up late every week partying with friends you have plenty of opportunity to see. That's not an exception, it's a lifestyle, and you must call yourself out and be honest. The goal you are working so hard toward every morning is worth more to you than staying up late. Likewise, if work is keeping you back in the office too many times each week, it's time to make a correction. When exceptions to your framework become the norm, call it out. Not doing so is being dishonest with yourself, derailing the goals that are important to making your life better.

PRACTICE BEING FLEXIBLE AND REJECTING PERFECTION

Always be aware of the dangers of overwhelm and burnout from placing too much weight on your shoulders because you demand perfection without flexibility. How can you be less perfection-oriented so you can accept a goal has been successfully achieved instead of continually scrutinizing and overly modifying it beyond realistic standards? In what areas of your life does striving to be perfect make you feel bad? Where do you need to be more flexible in your framework? When do you feel you take flexibility a bit too far?

Rule 10: Set Yourself Up for Success

It is often said that something is hidden in plain sight, and so, too, is rule 10: set yourself up for success. Because it seems obvious, this simple action is often unseen and undervalued.

You can think of this rule as an extension of rule 5—be prepared—and you can add it to every strategy in this book. To set yourself up for success, do whatever it takes to give yourself the best chance of succeeding. This starts with taking responsibility for your own self-improvement. No one but you can set you up for success. You are the only one who does the thinking that determines your actions.

Self-love is an important part of setting yourself up for success. Embrace your true self and promise that you will do right by yourself from now on. Trust yourself. Believe in yourself. Tell yourself, "I've got this!" Tell yourself that, no matter the temptation or struggle, you can overcome it and create a new life for yourself. This kind of positive, loving self-talk wards off self-sabotage, struggle, resistance, stagnation, and defeat. When we forget to love ourselves in everything that we do, we work against ourselves and set ourselves up for failure.

Once you've adopted this mindset, consider how to set yourself up for success in everything you do. This means taking actions that reduce friction and mitigate the risk of falling off the path or not working toward your goal. One way to do this is by maintaining peak health and fitness. Tired, unenergized people are less likely to have the determination necessary to get up early (let alone reach their goals) because fatigue lowers resolve. Set yourself up for success by going to bed early and looking after your health and fitness. Staying up late is self-sabotage. Smoking is self-sabotage. Excessive drinking is self-sabotage. Consistently eating fast food is self-sabotage. You get the idea.

Next, surround yourself with partners, friends, family, coworkers, and anyone else who supports you in your goals. They are your team. They will keep you accountable, offer you encouragement, give you guidance, motivate you, and help you through the good and bad times of the challenge you are stepping up to. After all, there is strength in numbers.

For those who are married or in a relationship, partners have a major influence on how we feel, the decisions we make, and our ability to take on any new habit. So do the people you live with, whether family members or friends. For that reason, we must get them on our side! Ask them for support. But keep this in mind: we are not preaching to them. Your aim is not to convert them into a 5 AMer. They don't need or want your persuasion to drink the Kool-Aid, yet they do need to understand what you're doing. Therefore, don't irritate them by jumping up and down, fist-pumping, and shouting with the excitement that you're, for example, using the power of physicality to activate your subconscious and become the world's greatest *whatever*. That's setting yourself up to fail. Quietly explain that you are practicing something new and that waking early is giving you the freedom to work on a specific goal you've been putting off.

That's all.

You may also consider engaging a coach. We are all aware of sports coaching. Yet most successful people off the field also take advantage of business coaching, career coaching, executive coaching, personal coaching, life coaching, guitar coaching, writing coaching, you name it. A coach on your team helps you succeed by saving you valuable time. Why waste a decade or more trying to figure something out when a coach can show you in a matter of months?

Always love yourself and be kind to yourself. Yes, you may have to have some honest conversations with yourself, as we describe in previous rules, but know it comes from a place of self-love, not self-hate. In fact, employing the 5 AM Advantage is in itself an act of self-love. You are taking an action to lead yourself to a better life. That is true love.

> ## PRACTICE SETTING YOURSELF UP FOR SUCCESS
>
> More often than not, it's up to you whether success is achieved or not, so it's critical to identify how self-sabotage plays a destructive role in your life. In what ways have you worked against yourself in the past? How can you now set yourself up better for success? In what ways can you love yourself unconditionally? How can that love help you achieve the goal you are working so hard to succeed in? How can you better set up all the other rules for the disciplined 5 AMer for success?

—

The habit of early rising is a powerful exercise in strengthening discipline because every morning we are tested. If we succeed in lifting the weight to successfully step up to that challenge, we become game fit, strong, and highly disciplined.

That is why the 5 AMer has the advantage—the ten rules for a disciplined 5 AMer not only help you master early rising but also help you master the activation of any goal you desire through discipline. Whatever the goal.

Of importance, all ten rules for a disciplined 5 AMer come from within— that is, they are rules of the 5 AM mindset. Therefore, goal activation, and the eventual success in achieving all goals, always comes from within. It always starts and finishes with thought. And when that thought is clearly directed with persistence, we can change the very fabric of our mental and physical being, as I outline in the next chapter, on the second goal activator of persistence.

Be prepared to have your mind blown.

CHAPTER 6

PERSISTENCE: THE SECOND GOAL ACTIVATOR

Success is not the absence of failure; it's the persistence through failure.
—Aisha Tyler, quoted in Alicia W. Stewart,
"Aisha Taylor's Recipe for Success"

Now that you understand how important the strong backbone of discipline is when it comes to successfully pursuing your goals, it's time to move on to the second goal activator: persistence. Recall from chapter 2 that persistence is the grit that keeps you going in the long term. Persistence is endurance. It's tenacity. It's the ability to steadfastly stay on your course of action for however long it takes, no matter the opposition. For the 5 AMer, persistence means taking one step at a time—continuing day after day—no matter what happened the day before.

As we learn in chapter 5, every morning is decision time, and if the right decision is taken, you are on your way toward successfully achieving your goal. But depending on your goal, the light at the end of the tunnel may be years away. Or you may never see the end of it, as your goal may be related to continual self-improvement. Persistence is what enables you to take the long-term view and not be dogged by it. Instead, you are driven by it, excited at the prospect of continuously practicing behaviors that will help you become the best version of yourself and attain the life you want. When you think long-term, dreams are less likely to be knocked off course by temporary slow-downs in momentum or inaction.

In this chapter, we explore what it means to take the long-term view and how you can learn to be more persistent with a basic understanding of neuroplasticity.

PERSISTENCE: A NEW PERSPECTIVE ON FAILURE

You're a 5 AMer. You are striving to wake up early every morning and work toward your goals to create the life you want. Persistence is what allows you to continue waking up at 5 AM to work toward your goals over the long term, even when faced with difficulties and opposition that threaten to—or do—knock you off track. When you're knocked off the track toward your goals, it can feel like failure. And failure is the ultimate discouragement. But when you develop persistence as a 5 AMer (as you will over your years of rising early), you realize that difficulties and opposition are temporary. They are not the end of your journey; they are part of your journey. The reality is that persistence only exists over the long-term. Understanding and embracing that gives you the advantage.

Persistence allows you to zoom out on your life. Instead of looking at your daily or weekly achievements, you view your progress over a month or even a year or more. When you do this, those so-called failures lose significance. If you mapped it on a chart, the overall trend would still be up, toward success (see figure 6.1).

We already know that failure is essential because it helps us find the strength that empowers us to climb out of the pit of despair. But now, with a long-term view of any goal, we can easily see that failure is a natural progression in an otherwise upward-trending chart. In other words, failure should be *expected* on the road to success.

That's not to say that a person cannot have a downward trending chart. As we've discussed, it's easy to do that when you're not taking control of your life. That's when moments of productivity are outweighed by self-sabotage,

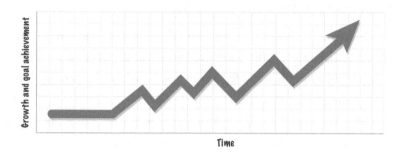

Figure 6.1: Upward-trending life chart of the 5 AMer

inactivity, and destructive behavior. It's when self-love may be lost. It may also be circumstances outside of your control that have derailed your upward trend—and you failed to correct course.

The 5 AM Advantage is a strategy to live an upward-trending life. Accepting failure as an essential and expected component of growth lifts us to a higher level, helps us exceed our old limits, and moves us beyond the boundaries of our comfort zone toward successfully achieving our goals. Failure, then, becomes a normal part of our story.

After more than five hundred emails, I failed to be picked up by a publisher. Yet these failures were priceless because they required me to embrace a more uncomfortable outcome than what I'd been planning for. And because I embraced the outcome before me—stepping out of my comfort zone by reexamining and rewriting the manuscript again and again—I was able to move past it and toward my goal. I was able to adjust, learn, and grow. I was able to persist.

Persistence helps us reframe what our inner voice tells us by redefining some of the words (such as *failure*) it typically uses to lead us astray. That way, we have a better conversation with our inner voice, one that encourages us to be persistent. Failure is no longer a disempowering force in our lives. From now on, when you hear or use the word *failure* or any other words that describe failure, anchor it to success, knowing this is a more accurate description as you persistently work hard each morning, rising upward on your life chart.

BITE BY BITE TOWARD SUCCESS

Desmond Tutu is credited as saying that "there is only one way to eat an elephant: a bite at a time." The 5 AMer has an advantage because we wake up each morning to work on a goal for one or two hours. In this way, we eat the elephant of our goal bite by bite.

However, our goals must be broken down into smaller bites, otherwise, we will choke. Intuitively, we know this. We read books page by page, lose weight pound by pound, and move to a new house box by box.

What's more difficult, however, is being persistent at working on those bites day after day and year after year. Fatigue is real. Becoming fatigued by unexpectedly long periods of persistence due to setbacks can make even small bites difficult to swallow. Therefore, even after you have broken a goal down into what you may consider achievable bites, you will invariably need to recalibrate because of setbacks. This means reorganizing plans, reprioritizing bites, discarding the old, adding new steps, and maybe even breaking it all down again. This is what allows you to adapt and grow.

These setbacks result in lost time, and therefore, an extension of your planned success date, making your goal seem that much further out of reach. This is where the previous goal activator of discipline is required to empower your persistence in working toward your goal. There *will* be setbacks. And some setbacks will push your endurance to the limits.

While writing this chapter, I talked to my old friend Milo on the phone. Milo asked me what I was up to. I hesitated before telling him I was writing my book. It had been nearly two years since we talked, and I still hadn't finished the book. I was embarrassed. I felt self-conscious. I felt judged. He asked how the book was going, and I explained that I had taken a long break after the bull accident and then struggled to get back into writing. I continued to explain that I also needed to cut out much of what I had previously written, as the past couple of years had given me time to practice, reflect, and gain greater clarity on my strategies. That was the most significant period of recalibration I experienced during the writing of this book. My date of success had been dramatically pushed back!

Milo paused and then said, "Well, you've certainly been persistent."

His tone was supportive and his comment timely, given the chapter I was writing. I felt a slight sense of tenacity, but my awareness of the passing of time jolted me all the same.

After the call, I went straight back to writing—yet now I was distracted. Earlier in the morning, my wife had also called, asking what I was up to. Fiona was away for a few days with our daughter, who was competing in a national horse-riding event.

Again, I hesitated before answering. I had been up since 5 AM, pounding away on my laptop. "Oh, I'm just doing a bit of writing," I said, downplaying it. There was a moment of silence on the phone. "I've also taken a few bookings for work and set up some new client accounts," I added quickly.

Although the call was pleasant, the years of recalibrating my goal of writing this book were wearing me down. My fragile writer's ego screamed, *She's frustrated that I'm still writing!* I had read her pause as a sign of disapproval—after all, she had caught me out writing again. So, in a panic, I camouflaged my *sinister* activity by adding some more acceptable work obligations and responsibilities into our conversation.

Now, totally distracted from writing, I opened the Finder on my MacBook and searched for my earlier manuscript files to confirm a few dates. The earliest date I had written notes about my 5 AM experiment was February 5, 2009. Over ten years ago, at that time!

"Fuck!" I said out loud.

At times, having the long-term, upward-trending view of a major goal seems impossible. There will be times when you're on one of those downward slopes. It may also seem you have flatlined. This was one of those times, and it hurt.

My spirit was crushed. I sat, thinking about a decade earlier when I had flown to Colorado to meet with a couple of coaches I'd engaged to help me publish what I thought was an okay manuscript. With their guidance, we had the manuscript edited and sent submissions to over two hundred and fifty agents and publishers—of which only one thought the manuscript was worth putting to print. My coaches recommended I not take up the publisher's offer; it wasn't a good deal and would result in a book that wasn't adequately developed, promoted, or supported.

I continued to work on the manuscript for a few more years, morning after morning. Finally, I engaged another editor to finish the now-retitled manuscript and submitted it again to more than 250 agents and publishers—without any suitable takers. I didn't have a quantifiable "platform," and these publishers were looking for a large tribe of followers ready to buy thousands of books.

Not ready to surrender, I had a book cover designed and was ready to self-publish when I was nearly killed by that bloody charging bull. After being physically incapable of doing anything with the book for over six months, I finally engaged another editor to help with the printing process. However, what I thought was a straightforward copy edit resulted in the entire manuscript being unformatted. To my horror, this removed every paragraph break, every section break, and some chunks of content. Pages that previously seemed so finished were lost without rhythm and flow—it was nearly impossible for me to recognize my own work.

Still, I persisted. I plunged into another rewrite. Only this time, I was in a state of physical and mental recovery from a major accident. Overwhelmed and aggravated by the state of my manuscript and my bull-induced PTSD, I burned out. I didn't touch the manuscript again for well over eighteen months.

Which brings me to today: rewriting this chapter, again. And the conversations with Milo and Fiona. And the conversation I was having with myself.

Being persistent is hard; there is no way I can sugarcoat it, and I still had another four years ahead of me. Working day after day, step by step over the months that morph into years that morph into a decade can be soul-crushing if you let it.

Yet my soul knows—and this is what you must learn, too—persistence is progress. Failing is progress because it requires you to recalibrate and grow. My long-term mindset allowed me to continue up the chart toward success, even after years of setbacks. It allowed me to look back at those earlier manuscripts as worthwhile steps on the path. I could have viewed the results of many of those steps as abject failures. I could have given up. Instead, my long-term thinking viewed them as temporary setbacks. What's more, those setbacks allowed me the time I *needed*. They allowed my research, practice, and writing experience to breathe and grow. If I had finished the book all those years ago, I wouldn't have fully tested the 5 AM Advantage in good times and bad, and the book would have fallen short of delivering its message.

Instead, the past decade of early rising and dealing with all of life's ebbs and flows gave me the experience I needed to successfully complete this project. I can see clearly now that those early pages are only scribbles, notes of ideas that needed to be tested, modified, and tested again and again over time. The work of my editors and the feedback from publishers forced me to recalibrate and reconsider better structures and strategies that had changed over the years. In other words, those setbacks were essential to my success.

REPETITION, REPETITION, AND REPETITION

The practice of waking at 5 AM allows you to practice persistence, just as it allows you to practice discipline. If you can persist at waking up early during the dark and dreary mornings of winter or when you lack motivation and simply think it's too damn hard, then you strengthen yourself to be persistent in anything you choose. That means any goal or dream is now possible, so long as you are determined.

There is another advantage the 5 AMer gains from persistence: repetition. You wouldn't be alone in thinking that persistence and repetition are one and the same. However, repetition relates to the act of doing, saying, or writing something again and again. If you look back to the description of persistence from a few pages ago, you will see a critical difference: persistence requires repeating thoughts and actions *steadfastly and despite opposition*. You persist in an intentional direction—upward growth—despite any setbacks.

Persistence, however, gains much of its significance from its repetition. Norman Vincent Peale, author of *The Power of Positive Thinking*, said that "repetition of the same thought or physical action develops into a habit which, repeated frequently enough, becomes an automatic reflex."[6]

---

6   Norman Vincent Peale, *Enthusiasm Makes the Difference* (New York: Fireside, 2003), 93.

This is critical to the 5 AMer because the repetitive aspect of persistence transforms you *mentally* by *physically* changing your brain, and this makes it easier to continue to be persistent to reach your goal. Instead of consciously making an effort to be persistent, it becomes second nature like breathing, something you don't need to think about.

This is the process of neuroplasticity. By harnessing it, the 5 AMer has the advantage of establishing the habit of waking up early to work productively toward successfully achieving a goal. It will become part of your physical makeup. The path to success will become automatic, long-lasting, and game-changing.

NEUROPLASTICITY

Every time you think or experience something, an electromagnetic, bio-chemical message travels through your brain on a set pathway along a series of nerves called neurons. Each neuron is an excitable nerve cell of the nervous system. They are found in a variety of shapes and sizes and are highly specialized for receiving and transmitting messages from one cell to another (see figure 6.2). All neurons have dendrites, branch-type extensions reaching out from the cell body, and a longer extension called the axon, which also has terminal branches at the end. This allows a message to move along a pathway from one neuron, out from the axon terminal branches, across the synaptic gap, and into the neighboring neuron via that cell's dendrites. As the message crosses over the synoptic gap, its action potential—that is, its ability to transmit information—is excited or inhibited by biochemicals released from neurotransmitters. Put plainly, these chemicals either speed up and "encourage" the signal or slow down and "discourage" the signal as it goes over the gap.

There are three well-known biochemicals that encourage neurological messages: dopamine, endorphins, and acetylcholine. Dopamine plays an important role in rewarding the neuron so we feel good; endorphins are produced in response to exercise and other stimuli to give us a euphoric high; acetylcholine has various roles including helping us focus, improve clarity,

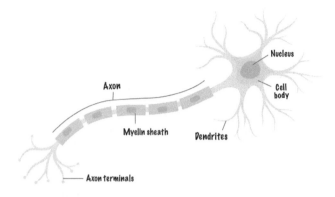

Figure 6.2: Neurons and the synaptic gap

and recall information. The 5 AMer harnesses neuroplasticity to use these three biochemicals to their advantage.

When messages travel along two neurons, they are said to be "firing together." As messages travel through the brain along millions of well-used pathways, brain networks are established. These networks determine the way we think, the actions that control our behavior, and the habits we acquire. All of which in turn determine who we are. But those pathways and networks can be changed. The brain can build new pathways and networks, which means we can change the way we think and act. This is the foundation of neuroplasticity.

HOW OUR BRAINS ARE SHAPED

The human brain is unique in many ways, including how sensory input influences the development of its structure and function. In other words, the environment we live in directly changes our brains during our lifetime and intergenerationally. Humans are also different from all other mammals in that we constantly and significantly shape and reshape the environment we live in, which in turn shapes our brains.

Let's take a quick look at our lives because we have all lived through one of the most dramatic periods of adaptation and environmental change in history. Technology is advancing exponentially—I only need to think back to my university days in the mid-1980s to see this. We punched paper cards that were used to enter data into the computer, which were later replaced by floppy discs. I can hardly remember the paper cards, and my kids have never even used a floppy disc. We have adapted and moved forward.

The smartphone took this change in environment to a new level. I remember trying to write my first text message, thinking it was too hard and would never last. Wow, how wrong I was! Smartphones are the most significant sensory input in our lives, and our ability to adapt to them is mind-blowing. Even my eighty-six-year-old mother has adapted and now relies on it every day.

If you think about someone who lived in 1824, two hundred years ago, their environment would be nearly unrecognizable: no electricity, no cars, limited education, few newspapers, delayed mail, and so on. The environment they lived in and the stimuli imputted into their brain was vastly different from the present day. If we time-warped a person from 1824 to today, they would surely have a breakdown from stimuli overload because we have adapted nearly beyond comprehension—and we have neuroplasticity to thank for it.

New experiences and new actions create new neural pathways and allow us to evolve thought processing unconsciously and without effort. For example, when you learn how to play a new instrument or learn to navigate a new city, new neural pathways are created.

However, it's not just external (extrinsic) input that can create new neural pathways in our brains. Internal (intrinsic) input such as an idea, inner dialogue, or thought can as well. This means we can use the principle of neuroplasticity to *intentionally* rewire our brains to our advantage. In this case, we are going to explore how you can intentionally rewire your brain to become more persistent.

FOUR RULES TO ENGAGE NEUROPLASTICITY

What does neuroplasticity really mean for the 5 AMer? How can we use it to our advantage to foster persistence? All you need to understand are the four rules of engagement.

Rule 1: Neurons That Fire Together Wire Together

We know an idea or thought (intrinsic input) and taking action (extrinsic input) connects new neurons, creating new networks. The more frequent these inputs, the more often the neurons fire together and the harder they become wired together—reinforcing and strengthening the pathway to create strong networks. Repeatedly using the same thought or action over time continually establishes even stronger networks that, in turn, make your thought and action easier, faster, and more automatic. The thought or act becomes habitual.

A 5 AMer intrinsically and extrinsically curates their environment persistently and repeatedly each morning by practicing their mindset and preparing their space for the work they need to do to reach their goal and take action. By design, your 5 AM routine utilizes the concept of neuroplasticity to make new and strengthen existing pathways in your brain—the pathways that will make it easier for you to achieve your goal.

The habit of waking up early, the skills you practice, and the constant pattern of thinking blaze along the same neural pathways morning after morning, becoming stronger and faster each time. Remember, the very first action of the day—waking up—represents the 5 AM Advantage as a strategy because it is an essential first step toward additional action and it requires the goal activators. In other words, the 5 AM Advantage prioritizes neuroplasticity, which grows those new mental networks.

By rewiring and strengthening your brain each morning, the 5 AM Advantage gives you the pathway to successfully achieve your goals and change your life. You have physiologically changed who you are and how you think. In other words, neuroplasticity allows you to *become* a morning person. More so, it allows you to develop the skill set of the person you want to be.

After practicing the 5 AM Advantage, I now have the skills and mindset to sit down and be a wordsmith, an author. This has taken a long time, as I was not a natural writer and did not do very well in English at school. But through repetition and persistence, I can now sit down and write out a page that reads okay. Likewise, I have also developed the discipline to dive into a freezing rock pool in winter in the dark of the morning. I practiced and gained skills that have formed new and stronger neural networks. It really is just a scientific process that we can harness to our advantage.

Rule 2: Gain Clarity to Free Yourself of Distractions

Paying close attention without distraction to a thought or task is essential for long-term brain adaptation. To get those neurons firing along a clear path, you need to keep your mind and thoughts on that path. In other words, if you are practicing an action or mindset and your goal is to strengthen neural networks, your focus should be 100 percent on the task at hand. Distractions, mind wandering, and similar interruptions disrupt the creation of the neural pathway or stop the neurons from firing together.

That's why waking up at the crack of dawn is so good for developing skills, persistence, and the other goal activators. The action of early rising and the work you do during your first hour or two is unlikely to be interrupted or distracted by the other demands in your busy life—that's why you implement it in the morning. It's a way for you to control your environment because most of the world is still asleep. You may still encounter intrinsic distractions, but you can tamp those down by developing your discipline.

During that early morning hour or two—before other work, before your partner wakes, before the kids ask questions, before your roommate starts banging around—you can focus on the challenge before you. More so, the first hour or two of the day is when your sleeping brain wakes refreshed from the night's mental processing. It's like a blank canvas, waiting for the artist to paint. So, when you seize this moment and take control of both your actions and thoughts, you not only have a jump on any physical extrinsic distractions but also have a jump on the mental intrinsic ones.

Some of you may think, "But this can be done any time of the day!" I agree. Some readers *can* change their environment and take action at any time to change who they are and successfully achieve their goals. But many others cannot. I've found that early mornings give most of us the best opportunity to control our environment and prevent distractions. If you do not find a space where you can gain clarity and focus, you will not reap the benefits of neuroplasticity, sabotaging your likelihood of success.

Rule 3: Reinvigorate Rewards

Rewards are a critical component of creating new neural pathways. Rewards are built into the system. When we create a new network and succeed in a task, we receive the reward of a hit of dopamine and acetylcholine. Dopamine, the "feel-good" hormone, reinforces that success as something you will want to do again repeatedly and persistently. Acetylcholine tunes us in to the experience, making a stronger memory. Our bodies do this naturally because they are designed to "reward" us when we are doing something that helps us survive from an evolutionary standpoint—eat, drink, reproduce, achieve goals, and so on. The biochemicals are what create the feeling of pleasure, and we want to repeat those behaviors.

You can amp up these intrinsic rewards by giving yourself extrinsic rewards, which we discuss in the previous chapter. Your body can release feel-good hormones both when receiving a reward and when thinking about future rewards. So, just as dopamine can get you to seek out a sugary snack, it can also get you to seek out and succeed in achieving goals.

As a 5 AMer, success in waking up early to work on a goal in the pursuit of living a better life rewards us because it activates the brain's two distinct pleasure systems. The first system is the pleasure we feel from thinking about the idea. Consider how much pleasure you feel when thinking about a new idea—a level of fitness you aim to achieve, the weight you vow to lose, a new model car or boat to buy, a house to own, or a holiday to go on. This type of pleasure is called *appetitive pleasure*. During these experiences, your body releases dopamine, making you feel excited.

You feel the second type of pleasure when using the idea—riding that first wave on a new surfboard, smelling the leather seats of your new car, and relaxing while drinking cocktails on your holiday island. This type of pleasure is called *consummatory pleasure*. During these experiences, the brain releases endorphins, giving you that euphoric and peaceful feeling.

While these experiences are still new and exciting, the neurons continue to blaze new pathways, competing with and occupying routes of seldom-used pathways and networks. Yet, over time, life goes on and your consummatory pleasure reduces. Boredom, dissatisfaction, and too much certainty reduce your body's need to release the chemicals until the feeling of pleasure no longer exists, or if it does, it has lost most of its attraction.

However, when a new idea sparks, the cycle of seeking pleasure begins again. Off go the neurotransmitter chemicals generated by appetitive pleasure, and you feel incredible. Remember, you're driven to actively seek what you crave; that is the nature of dopamine. The craving continues until you finally gratify what you desire. Then, *pow!* Your brain releases endorphins and activates your consummatory pleasure, and you feel ecstatic. Until that again diminishes.

This cycle happens in all aspects of life: new skills, education, love, relationships, sex, new toys, promotions, more money, or improving your life in myriad other ways. The cycle loops again and again throughout your entire life, from cradle to grave.

The strategy of the 5 AM Advantage utilizes this pleasure cycle every day. Appetitive pleasure happens when you're thinking about waking early the next morning, and consummatory pleasure happens once you awake and work toward achieving a goal. Furthermore, if you ever feel that boredom, dissatisfaction, or too much certainty is reducing your feeling of pleasure, persistently activating your goals (as I outline in this book) will help keep up the excitement and adventure of stepping up to a challenge, consistently reinvigorating your rewards system and stimulating neuroplasticity.

But thinking of new ideas and working step by step, day after day often becomes harder as we age. Does that mean an old dog can't learn new tricks? Does it mean that at a certain age, we need to just accept who we are and what we do—that it's simply too late? The answers are in the last rule for engaging neuroplasticity.

Rule 4: Use It or Lose It

Neuroplasticity is a competitive process because each new pathway is competing for pathways used by established networks. A repeated thought will claim the pathways of less frequently used thoughts, causing old networks to shrink and weaken from reduced and inconsistent mental activity. This is apparent when you forget a skill, memory, or thought not recently called on. In other words, when it comes to neuroplasticity, use it or lose it.

I may have played the guitar well thirty years ago, but seeing as I have not used those pathways for so long, newer skills have claimed the real estate. Today, it's difficult to pick up a guitar and play it. Some things I once knew how to play on guitar may be impossible now unless I decided to learn them again.

This change is continuous. Our brains are always adapting to newer and newer stimuli and environments.

It is true that when we're young it's easier to learn new skills. This is what Dr. Norman Doidge calls "the critical period" in his book *The Brain That Changes Itself.*[7] During these years, everything is new and exciting. New people enter our lives and we are learning how to crawl, walk, play games, talk, sing, and make music. The young brain has fewer networks, so there's little competition. We experience less inner dialogue, inner conflict, and external distractions, giving us greater clarity, more excitement, and more pleasure. Our neurotransmitters are exciting the synaptic gaps, as opposed to inhibiting them, and information is moving freely, efficiently, and abundantly. This builds new and strong networks—neuroplasticity is at its peak.

But as the years pass, we continue to create more and more networks that constantly need to be reorganized as they compete for space and attention. Little-used neuronal pathways must make way for new networks, so things aren't as free flowing as during the critical learning period. The effectiveness of the synaptic connections can now be inhibited by the neurotransmitters.

This all sounds like bad news, yet humanity could not advance without the capacity to inhibit, erase, or clear little-used pathways and networks. If

---

7   Norman Doidge, *The Brain That Changes Itself: Stories of Personal Triumph from the Frontiers of Brain Science* (New York: Penguin, 2007), 78.

not for the reorganization of neural pathways, we would all be stuck in the past, frozen in time, and unable to respond to new stimuli.

Luckily, the competitive nature of neuroplasticity is also critical in erasing destructive habits, unwanted memories, and negative patterns. As new and better pathways are made, those less-used ones start to weaken until they're relatively abandoned. You can take over those pathways that were once dedicated to a negative habit and replace them with something positive: either a new habit or the habit of *not* doing something. For example, a workaholic can learn to replace the desire to put in long hours in the office with the desire to spend time with his family. Even trauma and PTSD can fade when new thoughts and actions become dominant over time.

But how do we specifically use neuroplasticity to improve certain aspects of our lives, even when everything seems to be getting harder as we age? Unfortunately, life *can* become less exciting as we grow older. As we age, there is typically less true learning since we are mainly carrying out well-used learned skills such as reading, writing, driving, or working. Even when our work is challenging, requiring us to push ourselves to new extremes, it is only a variation of well-used skills in a job we've done for years. There's no spark. Nothing seems new.

The trick for the 5 AMer is making the old new again. Neuroplasticity is maximized when something important, surprising, or novel occurs, like when we experience passion and excitement or make an intentional effort to pay close attention to a new task or idea. This, of course, is baked into the 5 AM Advantage.

So, what type of person do you want to become? What do you want to do? What dreams, goals, and magnificent obsessions do you have? By prioritizing what you are passionate about and overcoming challenges by growing and learning truly new skills, you can use neuroplasticity to help you stay on track over the long term. In other words, you can boost your persistence. And you will succeed. Start climbing your upward-trending life chart to success.

—

As a 5 AMer, you practice being persistent each morning. The small steps you take repeatedly over the long term will bring success in achieving your goals in the long term. That success may come from blood, sweat, and tears, but it also comes from harnessing the science of neuroplasticity, allowing you to rely on fact and not faith.

To take this to the next level, we must focus on the job at hand because, where the focus goes, energy flows. In the next chapter, you learn to free yourself from distractions—for the rest of your life—and find happiness, health, wealth, and much more.

CHAPTER 7

FOCUS: THE THIRD GOAL ACTIVATOR

The successful warrior is the average man, with laser-like focus.

—Attributed to Bruce Lee

By now, you are developing the discipline and persistence to work toward successfully achieving your goals. But how many times have you been highly motivated to achieve a goal, only to give up as you got lost once again in the busyness of life?

Having read my accidental life journal, you know that I succumbed more than once to the busyness of life, which resulted in a life out of control until, at last, I finally asked, "Why did I get here?" Even though I was actively seeking direction and help, attending potentially life-changing programs, and reading potentially life-changing books, I still fell back into old routines without any permanent life change.

The reason most people don't achieve their goals isn't because they are beaten by the challenge itself. It's because distractions divert their focus on the work needed to achieve the goal. As you've seen, I've lived this reality myself.

That's why the third goal activator is focus. With focus, you keep your eyes on the target, you pay close attention, you concentrate, and you don't get distracted by anything outside that central point of activity. How? You will learn to eliminate distractions.

In this chapter, I outline two powerful tools—mind mapping and the 80/20 principle. I have used these over the years to develop better focus on working hard toward achieving my goals and living a better life overall. But before you learn those, you must understand what focus is and the risks you face from being distracted. Distractions can be very elusive, making them hard to avoid, often until it's too late.

FOCUS AND THE DANGER OF DISTRACTIONS

When you are focused, you direct your attention or concentration toward a specific object, thought, or activity. It is the ability to selectively attend to a specific stimulus while ignoring distractions. Focus is critical for achieving goals, completing tasks, and retaining information. When you use focus to concentrate your mental resources on a specific task, you can increase productivity, creativity, and overall well-being. You see why this is such an important goal activator.

But the first step in developing focus is understanding the enemy of focus: distractions. On the surface, distractions aren't complicated. There are two basic types: intrinsic (internal) and extrinsic (external). For example, right now I am at my home office desk. I could easily be distracted by intrinsic thoughts (*Wow, a swim over at the beach would be nice about now*) or extrinsic forces (someone knocking at the front door to sell me a new internet plan). Pretty simple.

The challenge is that distractions easily infiltrate the barrier of our focus when we aren't actively looking out for them. Most of the time, people walk through life with their guard completely down. And with the proliferation of technology, things have only gotten worse. The ding of our smartphones has trained us to flit our attention from one thing to another. This can be detrimental to finishing any type of work, let alone achieving your magnificent obsession. The antidote is simple: first, make sure you have a clear picture of what you are focusing on, and second, take stock of potential distractions so you are ready to bat them away when they come.

You've already done the first part. You identified your focus—your goal or magnificent obsession. The second part requires you to break distraction into two categories: the macro (big picture) level and the micro (small picture) level.

- *Macro level.* Ask yourself this question: "Does the way I'm living in general and the current direction of my life distract me from living a better life?" Consider both intrinsic and extrinsic factors. For example, does your work add to or pull you away from living the life you desire? Does your current level of health and fitness drag you down or energize you? Do your relationships work against you or help you become a better person? Is the fear of change holding you back from living life to the fullest? Are you being totally honest with yourself when deciding the direction your life is going? Is your outlook on the life you're living making you feel better or worse?

- *Micro-level.* Ask yourself this question: "What distractions am I at risk of at this moment?" You will likely need to take inventory of every small task that you do to work toward your overall goal. Again, consider intrinsic and extrinsic factors.

Once you identify distractions, you can take steps to eliminate them. The concept of waking up at 5 AM should eliminate some distractions—you are getting ahead of work demands, family commitments, and other responsibilities that consume your days. But there are other extrinsic distractions that you may be able to squash as well. Perhaps you will be working toward your goal in a noisy environment that has distracted you in the past. A solution may be to purchase noise-canceling headphones or scope out a new, quiet space to work in, such as a local library. I mention in an earlier chapter that I lay out everything I need to exercise in the morning, so I am not distracted by gathering items.

Intrinsic micro distractions—such as daydreaming or intrusive thoughts—can be a bit trickier to control, but you can overcome them with practice and discipline. Now, I can easily stop my mind from thinking about irrelevant things by reminding myself with intentional thought. I essentially remind myself of why my task is important and what is at stake. Every time a wandering thought comes into my head, I remind myself of the following:

- My reason for doing this—my why

- How great I feel working toward this goal—gratitude and contentment

- That when I keep achieving each bite, I must eventually achieve my goal—success

- What's at risk if I don't—danger

By using the rules of discipline, we have more than enough ammo to stay focused on our goals underway at this very moment. We work in the moment. We focus in the moment. Easy.

Unfortunately, macro focus becomes harder over long time frames because, even when you set the first hour or two of your day aside to work toward your goals, your focus is inevitably punctuated by the rest of your day. When you aren't or can't intentionally think about your goals, you relax, socialize, go to work, build a business, and meet commitments. You're at the call of others, you compromise, you reprioritize, and you abandon tasks. In other words, you are consumed by the busyness of your day. This is not unusual—such is life. However, it can be easy for the busyness of life to distract from the big picture, which is to live the *best* life possible. It can be easy to let the other major obligations in your life encroach on the time and resources you have dedicated to achieving your goals. If you need any reminding, reflect on your accidental life journal again to see all the distractions that have led you down the wrong path in life.

Distractions are cunning when you have your head down in the moment—day by day and year after year—microfocusing on the tasks at hand, thinking you are achieving success without realizing you are focusing on the wrong macro target. Remember, when I started Kindifarm, I genuinely thought I was combining my love of farming and animals with my desire to use my business degree. But the truth was, I had been motivated by a short-term entrepreneurial seizure to create a business, which I continued over many years as it allowed me to earn a living and support my family. That all clouded my judgment. I loved jackarooing, but that is not the same as teaching children about animals in the biggest city in Australia. Like a ninja move, all the blood, sweat, and tears from what had once been regarded as success, suddenly turned into a distraction. The city farm I had created suddenly became a major hindrance to living the life I desired. The goalposts had moved. Unfortunately, this switch usually takes place without notice, until that wake-up call occurs.

My accidental life was partially a result of not even knowing what my true direction was. I didn't know what I really wanted to do. I wasn't even clear about who I wanted to be! My goals were vague; therefore, the goalposts were not set. It was too easy to be distracted. In fact, I may have even liked the distraction. It meant I could avoid the harder questions and the bigger decisions. That's a danger we are all at risk of—so large and so in our faces, but we somehow still miss seeing it. Because we don't want to see it.

The rest of this chapter teaches you how to use two tools—mind mapping and the 80/20 principle—to reinforce big picture (macro) focus and the smaller bites (micro) that make up the big picture. Together, they will help you lead a life with fewer distractions.

MIND MAPPING

Mind mapping is an effective exercise used to organize and understand almost anything by creating a diagram that visually links thoughts, ideas, concepts, and pieces of information. Typically, a central idea or theme is placed in the center of the map, and branches radiate outward to connect related ideas or subtopics. Mind maps can be used for brainstorming, organizing information, problem-solving, and decision-making.

Mind mapping helps organize and structure ideas by visually connecting them in a non-linear way, allowing the brain to make connections between seemingly unrelated ideas, which can then stimulate creativity. This is because, as outlined by British author and consultant Tony Buzan in his book *The Ultimate Book of Mind Maps*, mind mapping encourages the use of both the left and right hemispheres of the brain, which can lead to more holistic and creative thinking.[8] The use of visual cues also helps make information more memorable and easily retrievable, which can lead to new insights and ideas.

For the 5 AMer, mind mapping is a great way to identify goals and break each down into smaller, more manageable bites, allowing you to better focus on each one as it comes instead of getting overwhelmed with the seeming enormity of the goal itself. We will also use it to blueprint our new abundant life (more about that soon).

I was first introduced to mind mapping in the mid-1990s, when I attended a program to help me better organize the structure and systems of my business. I used mind mapping to break down our operational procedures, which had seemed large and complicated, into smaller and smaller tasks that I could then delegate to a team member who could successfully execute them. This improved operations immensely, helping us eventually systemize the entire business, adding value that paid back in multiples when the business was sold.

Although Buzan popularized the term *mind mapping*, the practice of visually mapping out thoughts has been around for centuries. Today, it is used in many sectors of work for problem-solving, training, and goal setting, as well as with students and educators to map out study aids and lesson plans. Scientists and researchers use mind mapping to organize thoughts and experiments. The self-improvement and coaching sectors find mind mapping a valuable method to convey new strategies and concepts, and artists can use them to express ideas and stimulate creative flow. I even used mind mapping to initially plan out this book, allowing me to easily see the big picture before breaking it down into detail.

8   Tony Buzan, *The Ultimate Book of Mind Maps* (New York: HarperCollins, 2012).

We can use mind mapping to see the big picture goals (macro)—and your life—by visually organizing all its components (micro). I have used mind mapping software to create my maps as it allowed me to insert notes, display photos, use color codes or icons to prioritize ideas, and add hyperlinks to websites or files. This way, extra information was available without overcomplicating the visual aspect of the map. But I'm not solely recommending using software. More often, hand drawing makes it easier to access creativity and idea generation. There is also a risk of being distracted by learning and using the software itself. I now prefer to use butcher paper, Sharpies, and a whiteboard—although the back of a menu, napkin, or envelope works extremely well at a moment's notice. In any case, practice and see what works best for you.

THE 80/20 PRINCIPLE

Before we start mind mapping, it's helpful to gain a better understanding of how to best use your focus. After all, most of us don't have unlimited time to work toward our goals. To have the best chance at success, we need to focus on the work that will most likely get us to our goal. This is where the 80/20 principle comes in.

The 80/20 principle stems from observing what already occurs in the natural world and in our businesses, community, and society—there is an imbalance between consequences and causes. The principle states that about 80 percent of consequences come from about 20 percent of causes.

The 80/20 principle, more officially called the Pareto principle, is derived from the work of Italian economist Vilfredo Pareto, who observed that 80 percent of the land in Italy was owned by 20 percent of its people. Since then, the principle has been proven in many areas, including business management and mathematics. Some examples outlined by the already mentioned author Tony Buzan, and also by Richard Koch in his book *The 80/20 Principle*, include the following: Approximately 80 percent of a business's profits are derived from 20 percent of its customers. Approximately 80 percent of the faults in production come from 20 percent of the problems. Approximately

80 percent of the direction a business takes comes from 20 percent of the decisions. And so on.[9]

You can start to see where you might focus energy to gain the greatest return on effort (ROE). If we focus on the most valuable 20 percent of customers, profits can be increased. If we solve the most critical 20 percent of problems, 80 percent of the faults will be fixed. If we concentrate on the important 20 percent of decisions, business growth may multiply.

Then you can start applying the principle to other aspects of life to find guidance on how to spend time. If 80 percent of our happiness comes from 20 percent of what we do, then if we dedicate more time to the 20 percent, happiness will increase. If 80 percent of our day is taken up by 20 percent of the things we do, then we had better examine whether it's the right 20 percent. And if 80 percent of our achievement results from 20 percent of our efforts, we should focus on the 20 percent needed to achieve our goals.

Why the imbalance? Why doesn't 80 percent of your effort produce 80 percent of the results? No one really knows, but Vilfredo Pareto also noticed that 80 percent of the peas in his garden came from only 20 percent of the plants—so it's a reoccurring phenomenon both in the natural world and in the man-made world. In all cases, the inputs and outputs are simply not evenly distributed, and a small number of inputs are responsible for most outputs.

The key takeaway is that we can now use this to our advantage with outstanding results. To start with, I consider that small adjustment to a 5 AM waking time to be the 20 percent of input that results in large improvements to our life—80 percent returns.

After that, when we apply the 80/20 principle to all areas of our life, we can turn our lives around by identifying all those distractions that make up the 80 percent and instead focusing on the gold that makes up the 20 percent. That's when the magic happens, and we sort out the gold from the gravel to literally map out a new abundant life.

I have one last point, which I must add to prevent us from becoming

9   Richard Koch, *The 80/20 Principle: The Secret of Achieving More with Less* (London: Nicholas Brealey, 2007).

distracted by the numbers. Vilfredo Pareto also referred to the 80/20 principle as the *vital few* and the *trivial many*, meaning by focusing on those vital few and not the trivial many, large benefits result. In some areas of your mind map, simply focusing on the few and not the many is all you may need to do, instead of looking for the numbers.

YOUR NEW ABUNDANT LIFE

Reflecting on the moment when I decided to become a 5 AMer, I can clearly see that I drew a line in the sand. Leading up to that line, I was living an accidental life that was out of control, overwhelming, busy, suffocating, and stagnating. I was in that pit of despair that forced me to wake up, take action, and step over the line to start living my new abundant life.

I didn't take the decision to live a new life of abundance lightly. But the world we live in is abundant in everything we need. Our standard of living continues to grow year after year, we are living longer and healthier than ever before, and we have more opportunities to live how we want, do what we want, and be whomever we want. It's all available if we decide to step up and make the decision—to live a life of abundance; to be rich in health, happiness, time, freedom, family, friends, and wealth; to be in control. In that moment, I made the decision that from now on, I must intentionally live a life that was abundant, knowing with certainty that all I desired was there, waiting for me to claim it.

That makes it sound like changing the direction of your life is nice and easy. But drawing the line in the sand was only the first step. It took a few years for me to cross it, and it required all five goal activators, but focus was most important at that moment. The problem was that I couldn't clearly focus on what I wanted my new abundant life to be because of all the distractions from what felt like every area of my current life. The good and the bad. The pain and the happiness. Friends and adversaries. Profit and loss. My life was so disorganized—no wonder I didn't feel in control! With further reflection, it became clear that lack of control was the overriding pain I felt in life.

To live my new abundant life, I needed to get in control—and that meant getting organized. I decided to use mind mapping, as it had previously helped me in business. As I started, I didn't necessarily have a clear direction. I was just trying to wrap my brain around the complexity of my life at that date, get a handle on it, and (hopefully) find some direction and some control. But once the first draft was done, I could start to see all the components of my life at that moment clearly set out before me. Then, I knew I could continue working on cleaning it up to gain even more clarity that would highlight the decisions required to change and start living a new abundant life.

And this is what you're going to do now—map out the start of your new life of abundance.

In the following pages, I share excerpts of my own mind map as examples, just as I did with my accidental life journal. It shows my process of finding focus during periods of my life when mind mapping was critical to moving forward.

I recommend reading this chapter with a pen and paper so you can start getting a few broad ideas flowing. Then, I recommend you dedicate the next few early mornings to completing a detailed mind map. This will take effort, but trust me, it's worth it.

Like writing your accidental life journal, once it's done, you may never need to do it again. Creating this initial mind map will bring the areas of your life into focus so you can change them dramatically. The map ensures that this epiphany will not be lost to distractions as others may have been. If you have the map, you can always find your focus again. Step by step and goal by goal your life will change, and your mind map has worked—job done. However, you may decide to update your mind map on a regular basis, as required, to work on other areas of your life and new goals that you are ready to focus on.

Fully activating your goals with better focus through the following exercise in mind mapping and applying the 80/20 principle is powerful. However, continuing to practice mind mapping on a regular basis after finishing this book is a decision for you. From my experience, the advantages of drawing my initial mind map continue to this day as I think, plan, and make decisions with a greater degree of intention—improving focus. I now mentally place a new idea, option, or goal, into the original mind map. The imprint of the mind maps to memory is strong, and most details are easily recalled and used over again on demand. If I meet a new person, I know where they live on my mind map. If I'm considering a new activity, it has a place on my mind map. A new ache or injury even has its place. I then continue applying the 80/20 principle without having to physically carry out the exercise on paper. I have rewired how I focus.

Finally, as you go through the mind mapping exercise, you may think your mind map is incomplete, too basic, or not comprehensive enough to activate a change in the area being mapped. Don't worry, creative ideas are being generated even if they don't physically make it to the map. Intuitively, they influence your thinking and reflection. For me, I have not comprehensively mapped every improvement I would love to do on our farm, for example. However, the importance of focusing on the farm has become apparent—not to be overlooked in a busy life.

So let's get started.

HOW TO MIND MAP YOUR NEW ABUNDANT LIFE

In a nutshell, here are the four steps to creating your mind map:

1. Mind map every aspect of your life as it stands today.

2. Remove as many distractions as possible by applying the 80/20 principle.

3. Reflect on your newly decluttered mind map that is freer of distractions. And, where required, continue to mind map any idea, item, concept, component, desire, dream, goal, or magnificent obsession that you feel needs further breaking down into digestible bites, steps, or smaller goals.

4. If required, go back to step 2 and repeat.

To kick-start your creative neurons, draw a shape, such as a heart or whatever speaks to you, in the middle of a blank sheet of paper or whiteboard. Inside this, write, "My New Abundant Life." Remember, make it fun.

Mind mapping helps us break complex ideas—such as our vision for a new abundant life—into smaller bites to help us gain clarity on the big picture in the process. How can we break down our new life into smaller pieces? I recommend starting with what I call the foundations of your life, the things that hold it up, give it strength, and would contribute to instability if they happened to be weak. There are five foundations:

- Health and fitness

- Happiness

- Friends and family

- Wealth

- Work

You may discover different foundations as you get better with mind mapping, but in my experience, these five are a good place to start. Write them on your mind map and connect them to the center of your new abundant life, as I have done in figure 7.1, or in a way that resonates with you.

Remember, there are no hard rules with mind mapping. Creativity flows differently for us all. Don't be limited by my example or any of its components. The details of your foundations may very well differ from mine, or you may decide you want to mind map only one foundation at a time. For example, perhaps you already know that your health and happiness foundations are suffering more than others, so you decide to mind map those two areas of your life first.

No matter how you decide to mind map, don't succumb to analysis paralysis. Just start anyhow and see what the mind reveals. Don't worry about perfectly categorizing every component of your life—that's impossible. Perfection is the enemy. You only need a few gold nuggets that can change your life (remember the 80/20 principle).

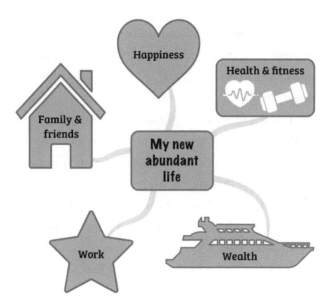

Figure 7.1: My foundations

By this point, your life may already be becoming clearer. You may also start to see, as I did, that certain areas are going to require more focus than others. It's also possible you may realize that your foundations are interconnected. For example, I realized happiness is closely linked to work. But don't let any of those thoughts bog you down. That's the creative energy starting to flow.

Now that you have a broad overview of your life, you can start focusing on each foundation in more detail. To do this, you are going to follow a strategy that I liken to throwing down all your cards on the table so you can pick up the aces. To show you how, I'm going to break down how I fleshed out each of my foundations, starting with health and fitness.

Foundation 1: Health and Fitness

To successfully achieve my goals, I knew I needed the energy to stay invigorated and maintain momentum over time. I knew I could only achieve this if my level of health and fitness was high.

Most of us know what must be done to keep ourselves healthy, yet this foundation is often put on the back burner, conveniently forgotten, or depri-oritized. We cannot delay good health and regular exercise until "someday." It must be given priority in life, otherwise, a health crisis will force a change—but it may then be too late.

In my early thirties, the years of physical labor lifting farm animals, haul-ing bags of feed, and doing general farm maintenance damaged three of my lower discs, which would bulge and put pressure on my spinal cord, resulting in excruciating pain. One morning, when putting my socks on (of all things), a pain like a bolt of lightning forced me to the floor. After seeing a back spe-cialist, he gave me two options—three months of back rehabilitation sessions or back surgery. I chose rehabilitation.

Being overweight has never been an issue for me, but as I started rehab, I noticed that most of the patients in their sixties or later were overweight. Over the weeks, it became clear that their baseline level of health and fitness was so low that it made rehab a very slow and painful exercise. In fact, it often ended in an unsuccessful return to wellness and a lifetime of feeling unfit, unhealthy, inflexible, tired, and listless. This was a huge wake-up call for me. And so I made a vow that as I aged I would do so in good health and fitness—that was priority one.

After rehabilitation, I joined a local gym and continued my routine of working out three times a week. A friendly man named Leigh owned the gym with two of his sons. He was in his sixties but, by contrast, was extremely healthy and fit. And to top it off, he was very happy. Over the next five years, Leigh and his sons helped me realize that by maintaining fitness and body strength, my back pain could be minimized if not altogether cured. This regular fitness regime gave me improved energy, productivity, and happiness.

I have a friend with similar back pain. I shared my story with him and assured him that if I could commit to fitness—even at the beginning when I ran multiple businesses, was parenting three children, and was maintaining a social life with a new partner—then he could, too. But health is not his prior-ity. So he smokes, overeats, overworks, and does little exercise. Sadly, to this day, nothing has changed. When he visits our farm, without fail, he spends the evening on the floor in front of the open fire, plagued with excruciating back pain and barely able to move from the exhaustion of an active day. He doesn't see how work—his big distraction—affects his life, taking priority over health because his measurement of success is largely money.

I love my friend dearly and share this story not to shame him but to give a warning: no one can force life choices on you, not even your best friend. It must always be your own decision.

Still, many of us think it is acceptable to stop exercising and eating well when life gets too hard. A work deadline often seems to give us permission to skip the gym or our daily walk. The responsibility of raising a family may excuse us from keeping fit and healthy. When the pressure is on, we drink more, smoke more, go without sleep, and worse still, believe it's acceptable—even admirable—to abuse ourselves in the name of meeting commitments and maintaining hard work ethics.

Sadly, these exceptions often become habit, jeopardizing our well-being and life.

Instead, we must take ownership of our health. When there is increased demand for psychological and physical energy (such as working persistently toward achieving your goals), then we must stay fit and healthy. For peak performance, we need to eat well. Our body requires a well-balanced diet to function efficiently. When working hard, we need sufficient sleep to rest and repair the body and to take on the next day with vigor. To consistently perform at our best, day after day over months and years, we need to maintain energy and stamina. We all need to be world-class athletes (in our own world).

If we are to achieve our dreams, we need to be clear about what's required to keep us healthy and fit. Start to map your health and fitness foundation, using an excerpt from mine (see figure 7.2) as an example.

First, what health and fitness issues are distracting you from living the best life possible? Don't make this complicated—branch out anything that is making it hard to bounce out of bed and achieve your goals with vigor. For me, there were a number of medical appointments I needed to schedule, a lack of gratitude, and maybe a few too many beers on a Friday night. Next, branch out everything you could do to improve your fitness; I simply called this "staying active." Then, branch out all the ways you could do that. Don't

Figure 7.2: Mind map for the health and fitness foundation

limit yourself. Include anything you think would be fun that will keep you fit—many will directly help eliminate or at least reduce those distractions. Don't worry if you feel you are repeating yourself; it's all part of the process and clarity will come.

On the health side, diet is always an area that can be improved on, so branch out various ways to eat and drink better. What do you need to start avoiding? Sugar? What medical checkups do you need (given your age and environment) that may help catch any unknown issues early? I have an annual blood test that can check cholesterol, cancer, and other diseases. What existing health issues or injuries (like my back injury) do you have? What is required to fix them? Does your family history have any health issues that need to be checked? (My family has a history of thyroid problems, so I accounted for that.) Are you the correct weight? And so on.

Go all out on your health and fitness mind map, and remember the 80/20 principle: If 80 percent of feeling physically or mentally unhealthy, sick, or in pain is a result of 20 percent of the causes, what are those two or three factors that will change your life when improved? To answer this, you may need to branch out areas to research and seek help from doctors and specialists. For me, it was lens replacement surgery on my eyes to remove the need for glasses, having a few skin sunspots treated from years of working outdoors, and modifying my diet to reduce cholesterol after having my blood tested.

In any case, again, don't be distracted by the numbers, the 80/20. You know there are at least two or three activities you can start doing that will improve your fitness. I started by simply walking on the beach, and before I knew it, I was jogging. You also know how to eat and drink better—please don't make it complicated. Over time, you can fine-tune it as your knowledge improves through research and results. For now, simply ticking, crossing, or making notes to highlight those few ways you can improve your health and fitness allows you to add them to your framework. Remember, small bites will bring large results when persistently carried out over the long term.

After mind mapping and applying the 80/20 principle, break each item down so you can gain clarity and focus on your goals free of distraction. Ask yourself: How fit do I want to be, and how will that be measured? For me,

I want to swim at least one and a quarter miles a week over two mornings, go to the gym twice a week, and jog between three and five miles one day a week, depending on the tides. So I added those goals to my mind map. Start asking questions. What weight do I want to attain? What health practices do I need to make lasting habits?

The most effective way to stay fit and healthy is to participate in activities you enjoy. Surfing, jogging along the beach, and swimming in the rock pool are my preferences. I'm in this for the long haul, and I visualize continuing those activities well into my older years. Why not do something you love?

Focusing on your health makes you feel better and less distracted by issues that are robbing you of your life. The advantage of being a 5 AMer is that your wellness can take priority in your day if you decide it will. There is no better time than the first hour each morning to practice better well-being, remove any distractions, and successfully achieve your goals.

Foundation 2: Happiness

Happiness affects all areas of your life, especially the progress and likelihood of achieving success. When you're happy, it's easier to spring out of bed and work productively toward your goals. When you're happy, you have a positive mindset and are more likely to remain persistent in the challenges before you. When you're happy, you're highly creative, effervescent, and inspirational. When you're happy, life is great!

But life is not always happy; nor should it be. Sometimes, it seems like people believe true happiness is *continual* happiness. But this isn't realistic, and this expectation can be devastating, setting us up for extreme unhappiness when things inevitably go wrong or become difficult. Failure is important because it helps us learn and grow. Likewise, unhappiness is a healthy part of life. Understanding that it's okay to feel unhappy—and that it will pass—is essential.

The value of unhappiness, like failure, may at times be hard to appreciate, but it's a red flag of sorts, and we must learn to recognize it. Often, it's a signal for us to rest, change something, or seek improvement. In many ways, unhappiness is a call to action. Ongoing unhappiness may signal that we require help from a peer, coach, therapist, or doctor.

Besides, how do we know what true happiness is unless we have unhappiness to compare it to? One doesn't exist without the other.

Although excessive levels of happiness are unsustainable, unrealistic, and detrimental, you can reset your expectations to be happier more often than you're experiencing now. This is great news—particularly if you're experiencing periods of unhappiness that are distracting you from stepping up to your goal. That would be an intrinsic macro-distraction.

Let's mind map happiness to discover what makes us happy and what doesn't to increase our level of overall happiness. After all, we love ourselves; shouldn't we be happy? Start with two branches, one for *happy* and one for *sad* (see figure 7.3).

Mind map everything that makes you happy, and then map what makes you sad. Don't hold back. This is your chance to expose all those things that really tick you off and all those things that fill you with incredible joy. For me, feeling trapped and knowing I could be living a better life forced me to break that idea down. One thing that came to mind was simply that my business was a seven-day-a-week operation. In fact, weekends were even busier than weekdays. And after seventeen years (at that time), I was exhausted and totally over it! On the flip side, walking along Narrabeen Beach shortly after 5 AM before a swim in the surf was really making me happy. The sight of the sun rising slowly over the horizon, the sound of the waves and seagulls, the smell of the salt air—it was one of the happiest experiences of my life!

Now, let's reflect on the 80/20 principle. If 80 percent of happiness comes from 20 percent of your activities, what are those 20 percent? And if 80 percent of your unhappiness comes from 20 percent of your activities, what are those 20 percent?

To put this into practical terms, remember the vital few and the trivial many. Choose the two or three things that bring you the *most* happiness. These are going to be the few activities you focus on that greatly increase your overall feelings of happiness. Next, on your mind map, tick or make notes

Figure 7.3: Mind map for the happiness foundation

to highlight a few areas you can work on that will make a difference. You can even brainstorm strategies on the mind map. For me, I decided to focus on gratitude for all the amazing things I have in my life and to make more magical moments like taking everyone to the movies, riding motorbikes at the farm with the kids, enjoying a cool drink with my wife at the end of the day, and watching the horses and cattle in the paddocks as the sun sets. It's not that complicated—when you're not distracted.

Once you finish with *happy*, move on to *sad*. Identify the two or three bites that make you the most upset, and then brainstorm actionable strategies that reduce those things in your life. Like me, you may find this process harder than that for happiness, which is counterintuitive because we tend to focus on the bad things more. However, it can be hard to break down big problems—like feeling trapped in life—into smaller bites that are easily actioned. After breaking down working seven days a week, I found what made me unhappy was my requirement to always be at work. I needed to make sure all four vehicles (mobile farms) left with the correct gear and animals on time and to care for the other animals left behind, needing to be fed their bottles of milk. So the real thing that made me sad was my staff not doing everything required when I wasn't there. No wonder I felt trapped! I decided to add a checklist (which I mind mapped) for staff who worked on the weekends, which mostly eliminated my requirement to work Saturdays and Sundays. The problem that made me unhappy—supervising staff—was relatively small. However, until then, it was ruining my weekends and contributing to my overall burnout. The checklist was a small improvement with large benefits. I also outsourced accounting, which I hated doing, and reduced my exposure to a few destructive people in my life (I talk more about that in the mind map for family and friends).

Speaking of other foundations, don't worry if you have the same item in multiple foundations. You'll see that some health-related items—such as checkups—are on this map and the health and fitness one. That's perfectly okay, and in fact, it's highly beneficial because seeing something appear in different areas of your life highlights it so you're more likely to take action.

There is nothing difficult about this process. Its simplicity is its advantage.

How easy is it to do more of the things that make us happy and less of the things that don't? It's that simple—let the nature of the 80/20 principle proceed.

You may be wondering about the 80 percent we have now decided not to focus on. It's a good question—especially with the foundation of happiness. We often look for happiness in all the wrong places: shoes, clothing, a bigger house, a perfect marriage, well-behaved children, a dream job, a large paycheck, an overseas holiday, more free time, a million likes or followers, greener grass, and a body that belongs in the next blockbuster movie. These are all distractions! Beware! They will rob you of your happiness. That's the 80 percent that only brings 20 percent of your happiness. That's not how you seek happiness in your new abundant life.

The same goes for the things that make you sad: traffic, bad weather, a rotten movie, politics, the news, cleaning the bathroom, taxes, a bad word spoken without real contempt, a hot coffee served warm, slow internet, a delayed flight, or lost keys. These are the trivial many that aren't the root of your real unhappiness. When you focus on eliminating the vital few, these trivial many won't tend to worry you so much.

Foundation 3: Family and Friends

Successfully achieving your goals requires the support and encouragement of your family and friends—your community. It's impossible to be successful in isolation. Paradoxically, family and friends expose you to great risk because they can unintentionally (or intentionally) distract you from successfully working toward goal achievement by sabotaging, oppressing, or confusing you.

The purpose of mind mapping our family and friends is to prevent being distracted by people who drag us down and to gain strength by building a team who will cheer us on, no matter how hard life may feel at times. Mind mapping also enables us to gain clarity about the roles other people play in our lives, so we are not confused by misconceptions about how we should react and behave around them. After all, interacting with people can be hard, so now is the time to make the framework that will make those exchanges better.

Family can provide us with the strongest direction in life, helping pave the way into our future. As children, we rely on our parents, siblings, or other relations to show us how to live and act, until eventually, we enter the big wide world as young adults. That guidance shapes who we become, and this continues over our lifetime. I'm in my fifties and I still learn from my mother, now in her eighties. She's not teaching me how to clean my bedroom. Now, it's how to deal with the inevitability of old age, how to come to terms with our mortality, unrealized dreams, and the importance of family love. This is not a lecture—she teaches by example. I have felt the pain when her active days growing flowers on her small farm ended and the hard decision was made to sell the land. She once said, "Time beats us all."

Friends also give us direction. In our childhood and youth, we seek and attract new friends like magnets, sharing new experiences together in the schoolyard, university, workplace, sporting events, bars, and so on. New friends help us cope with an unfamiliar and uncertain environment. Life marches on, and if those friendships remain symbiotic—both individuals giving and receiving—they continue. If, however, the giving or receiving becomes unbalanced, the friendship may be jeopardized and feelings of help and support replaced with loss and hurt. Sometimes friends can be destructive—distracting us from living the best life we can and from achieving our goals. Even the strongest and most intense bonds of friendship can be left behind, and new bonds can be formed. This is how we adapt. But this can be confusing.

The bonds of family are usually stronger than friendship, but in practice, this is not always the case. That is why this foundation includes both. Friends and family can equally support or distract us, and now is the time to gain clarity by focusing on who's important to us and who isn't. As you create your own mind map of this foundation, use the excerpt from mine (see figure 7.4) as an example.

Out of all five foundations, family and friends can feel a little uncomfortable and insensitive to mind map. Living in a civilized society, we have been taught to have manners and be polite. So let's be clear: I'm not asking you to be abusive, impolite, or insulting to the people in your life. This map

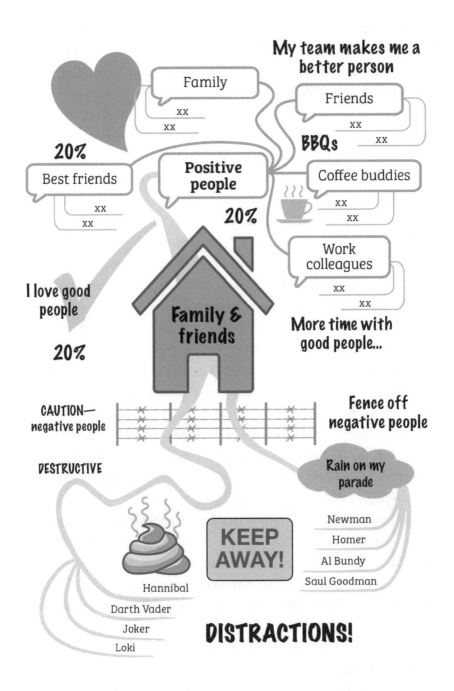

Figure 7.4: Mind map of the family and friends foundation

is for your eyes only. Yes, the mind map is extremely private and sensitive, but this is a process of bringing those who love you closer and moving those who don't further away. If someone notices that change, it may need to be addressed with them, or it may not. Either way, the intention is to help you live a better life, and if that requires stepping out of your comfort zone to let go of someone, it may be that time.

Accordingly, as I continue with notes from my own new abundant life mind map, I'm not using real names or going into any detail beyond giving you guidance. For starters, I suggest you branch out from your central idea of family and friends to two critical groups that identify anyone *not* helping you live a great life. This will require you to be totally honest in your assessment, which can be challenging because no one is perfect. (If perfection is your criteria, you will live a lonely life.) However, some people really do need to be called out.

So the first group is for people who are outright harmful to your happiness, progress at work, health and fitness, finances, goals, dreams, magnificent obsession, or in any other way whatsoever. Name this group: destructive.

Second, list anyone who regularly rains on your parade. That might be someone who often, but not always, is overly critical of you. Name this group (just for fun) "rain on my parade." But to be serious, a sideways glance or negative undertone can derail the best of us. So the first group includes people you must avoid whenever possible, if not altogether, and the second group includes people you must see less, at the very least. On my mind map, I have overextended a thin branch leading to both groups, the most destructive being at the outer reaches of the mind map, emphasizing the necessity to distance myself from them.

I have, however, used shorter, thick branches to closely connect to those who help me live a better life—those who help me reach my goals—as I consider them to be on my team. Even this simple distinction of distancing or closely connecting different people can greatly increase your likelihood of being persistent in working toward your goal.

Next, extend branches out to other groups as your situation determines to give you clarity as to what role these people play in your life. For example, it's fine to have friends whose role in your life is no more than someone you stop for a quick chat with (e.g., your neighbor or someone you often see at the local shop). Confusion and distraction result in thinking that person should go beyond their role by inviting you to their next party, for example. When the party is underway, but your invitation never arrived, you may start asking, *Am I not good enough? What have I ever done to them? Why don't they like me?* And on and on. Simply clarifying the role of people in your life gives you certainty and reduces confusion. I'm now more than happy to have a chin-wag with passing friends for a minute or two without feeling the need to invite them over for a barbecue—it's totally okay.

How many groups of people do you have? Don't worry if some people end up in more than one group. Someone in your closest group can also be one of your training buddies.

Once you have an idea of the people in your life with a family and friends mind map, it's time to apply the 80/20 principle. We enjoy 80 percent of happiness, support, understanding, connection, love, appreciation, encouragement, and so on, from 20 percent of the people. Identify those 20 percent. These are the people you need to spend more time with. Come up with actionable strategies that help you create that time. For example, if you identify a long-standing friend as part of that 20 percent, make a plan to spend more time with them. Again, don't become distracted by numbers—seek the vital few. If one or two people are really helping you get fit, train more often with them. If someone is supporting your business ideas by inspiring or motivating your efforts, meet with them more often. You can add those strategies anywhere on your mind map or simply acknowledge them so you see them.

The emotional ties of family and friends can be very strong, but your best friend at age eight may now, at forty, give you only grief and confusion. Be honest as you evaluate relationships because you may have unreasonable expectations from people, thinking they should be good friends when, in fact, they are not. Likewise, you may not be investing enough time in your strongest allies.

Overall, the goal is not to always fully eliminate the 80 percent—it's to spend more time with the vital few. For sure, destructive people must be eliminated from your life whenever possible. But you don't live in isolation and, overall, most people contribute to the broader community in which you live. The aim is to simplify your relationships to be free of distractions.

There's one last point I need to make. At the beginning of this chapter, I mention that you may feel your map is incomplete. This may particularly be the case with the foundation of family and friends. Rest assured, I didn't include every person in my life. I mainly focused on people who would help me, were destructive, and those whose role in my life confused me and, therefore, distracted me. After doing this map once, I see the need to distance myself from someone when I notice them having a negative effect on my life. I don't feel I must physically update my map because the imprinted memory serves me to this day, but you may update it. On the flip side, if I feel a good friend is becoming distant, usually because we don't live close to each other, I reach out and reconnect to maintain that beneficial vital few.

Those few acknowledgments will make a big difference. After all, having an abundant life with great family and friends who help and encourage your efforts makes achieving goals more likely, and it makes life more enjoyable. It's that simple. But, even so, this can be one of the hardest foundations to get right, so I know this will help.

Foundation 4: Wealth

Wealth is an exciting foundation to mind map; it's often a favorite of my coaching clients. However, you will see that while wealth is a powerful source of motivation—a carrot—it is also a major distraction.

To achieve our goals, we need to be clear about our real aspirations in this crazy world of consumerism, one in which we are constantly told that wealth brings happiness and that a person's ability to accumulate money is the ultimate sign of success. The paparazzi feverishly follow the rich and famous, providing up-to-date and sometimes hourly accounts of how these people—Jeff Bezos, Elon Musk, Bill Gates, and the like—live. Each year, magazines publish lists of the richest men and women, placing them on winners' podiums. It's easy to start believing that life is one big race to the top of the money pile.

We need to be aware of how we think about wealth. It's too easy to become victim to the illusion that we need tens of millions of dollars to have all we want in life and without that huge amount, we cannot be happy or worthy. Being bombarded with these astronomical figures can make us feel depressed when we fall short of those inflated figures in our own life. Interestingly, a 2019 study by Nobel Laureates Daniel Kahneman and Angus Deaton found that happiness increases with wealth at a diminishing rate as income climbs to $75,000, and then stops altogether.[10] A 2020 study by Matthew Killingsworth suggests that it may indeed continue after that level of wealth. However, unless you really value money, it's not by much.[11]

The purpose of mind mapping wealth is to gain clarity of what things we *want* in life (things we desire) over what we *need* (things which are essential) to stop being distracted by this illusion that we must have vast wealth to be successful and happy.

First, there is no doubt you can have everything you *need*: a house to live in and provide your family with shelter, security, and a nurturing environment; food on the table; clothes that protect you; and a car to provide transport. The utilitarian view of what we need is not sexy, and it can become boring, so the lines between the things we need and the things we *want* easily become blurred. Clarity is lost, and then confusion and distraction set in.

In this mind map, you are only going to focus on wants. This will help you determine how far you should go in search of wealth. When is enough enough? If you don't understand this, you risk the pursuit of money being a distraction in successfully achieving goals. If we are to move forward with our goals, wealth is best used as a source of motivation, not a distraction.

However, clarifying what we want in the first place is the hard part. Most

---

10 Daniel Kahneman and Angus Deaton, "High Income Improves Evaluation of Life but Not Emotional Well-Being," *Proceedings of the National Academy of Sciences* 107, no. 38 (September 2010): 16489–16493.

11 Mathew Killingsworth, "Experienced Well-Being Rises with Income, Even above $75,000 per Year," *Proceedings of the National Academy of Sciences* 118, no. 4 (January 2021), https://doi.org/10.1073/pnas.2016976118.

of the time, we think we want something when we don't. The mind map will help us clarify what it is we want and what is simply a distraction—something that is taking up valuable thinking space when we could be focusing on the 20 percent of wants that will benefit us.

To do this, we are going to have a lot of fun by imagining that you have an open checkbook. It's time to buy everything you have ever wanted, no matter what! To start, branch out from your foundation of wealth with any major group of items you would love to buy (see figure 7.5). You might have a group for your new house, another for travel, another for toys (cars, boats, helicopters, etc.), maybe a group for your wardrobe, one for holidays, and so on. You may even like to make a wish list so you can go all out and imagine anything is possible.

Remember, there are no limits—it's time to go shopping, and you don't have to think about the bank balance. Mind map everything you have ever dreamed about or wanted to buy. And I mean *everything*. Enjoy the process!

A significant shift often occurs when mind mapping wealth, and it annoyed me at first. We start to run out of things we want to buy sooner than we thought—way sooner. In fact, most outrageously extravagant items don't even tend to make it onto the map. How strange! One reason for this heartening lack of greed is that we all have an intuitive appreciation of the cost to buy these possessions. As we go through this process, this intuition is expanded when gaining clarity around the amount of money and, therefore, the amount of effort, energy, and focus needed for the purchases (even though I clearly said you had an open checkbook). Once I accepted the reality that I didn't desire owning an entire desert island or a Learjet, I was no longer annoyed by my lower ambitions of wealth. I had learned a valuable lesson.

Anything that requires too much return on effort—energy, hard work, focus, time away from your family, impact on your health and happiness—is a distraction!

Suddenly, it becomes clear that the $10 million yacht requires us to make too big a commitment that would mean missing other things in life that make us happy, healthy, and connected to our loved ones. All those other things in life *are* more important. This is a great starting point.

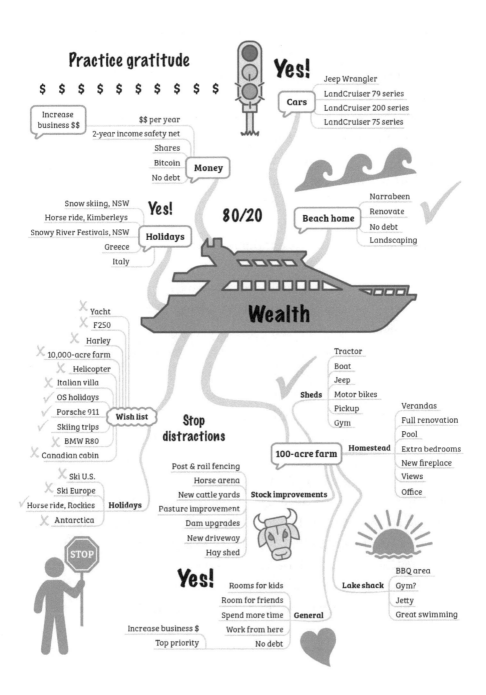

Figure 7.5: Mind map for wealth

But where do you set that limit? Well, it's not really a limit. I'm not suggesting you limit your thinking. You may desire a Learjet, and even if you don't, after successfully achieving many of those smaller bites and bigger goals, a Learjet may move into your focus. But for most of us, today it isn't on the list. And that's the power of this mind map. It keeps the focus on all those smaller bites and goals you have decided to work hard toward achieving.

Even if the desert island didn't make it onto your mind map, let's remove as many distractions as we can by using the 80/20 principle. Consider the return on effort for each item, knowing you derive 80 percent of your happiness, contentment, self-worth, pride, love of life, and so on, from 20 percent of your possessions. Cross out anything you simply want to stop wasting time thinking about. Highlight the 20 percent and tag anything you may want to keep as a future goal but not be distracted by today. In my own wealth mind map, I would love ten-thousand acres of prime cattle country with a large homestead and all the extras. However, once I considered where my four children live and go to school, my wife, how I earn my income, my age, and how long it would take—it's not what I decided to focus on. Had I possessed this clarity twenty-five years ago, it may have been my focus, but now in my fifties, it's not. This is the value of mind mapping wealth: beating myself up over why I'm not living on a vast cattle property would be a *major distraction*. Especially when I already own a beautiful hundred-acre cattle farm within two hours of all my children and our family home by the coast—that's where my focus needs to be. Therefore, I crossed out the ten-thousand-acre cattle property on my mind map.

Without clarity of what wealth means to us, distraction robs us of focus. With clarity of what wealth means to us, we gain gratitude. Practicing gratitude is critical because it helps us lead a more fulfilling life while improving our mental health, happiness, well-being, and self-esteem.

Now that we've removed the distractions (and found gratitude) we can focus on our goals and mind map all the steps required to successfully achieve them. It may be beneficial to pull out the calculator and physically add up the value of all the items that now remain on your mind map. It may surprise you how affordable your idea of wealth is now. This is when wealth becomes a powerful motivator. You can now include plans to achieve that 20 percent.

I wanted to own both our house by the coast and the hundred-acre cattle farm, without a mortgage or debt. That would give me a substantial level of wealth (as per my mind map) and also tick other boxes such as happiness, security, less stress, and so on. Becoming debt-free required achieving other goals, too, such as increased business turnover and profit level. Morning after morning, bite by bite, goal by goal, and with focus, the debt was repaid. Importantly, overwhelming debt was a major distraction during my accidental life. Living debt free is my new abundant lifestyle. I'm living on the correct side of that line I drew in the sand. That's the 5 AM Advantage.

This is a mind map that you can come back to over the years as goals are achieved and you climb, one bite at a time, that upward trending chart. Over time, through persistence and all the goal activators, you will regularly gauge which return on effort is worth it. For example, can you move from a small but comfortable house to a larger home or better location without it becoming a distraction? What return on effort to upgrade your car is beneficial to your requirements before it becomes a distraction? What return on effort makes booking your next holiday achievable before it becomes a distraction? In many cases, the return on effort is simply not worth it.

By focusing on wealth, we gain control. When the pressure has been removed and you are no longer stressing or feeling worthless over things that are no more than distractions, your mind's neural pathways improve to focus on the things that *do* matter.

The advantage of being a 5 AMer is that you now have time to be grateful and consider what wealth truly means to you. You can decide how much you need, by what means, and how long it is going to take to accumulate. By mind mapping and applying the 80/20 principle, you decide with certainty what level of wealth you really desire and can then work productively toward it.

Foundation 5: Work

I mention at the beginning of this chapter that there is never a clear-cut separation between foundation boundaries, and this is most apparent with the foundation of work. The purpose of mind mapping work is to gain clarity about how your work contributes to your new abundant life (or doesn't).

To start, I would like to reflect on my days working at Kindifarm, which also included taking our menagerie of farm animals to nursing homes (my favorite visits, by the way) to give the residents diversional therapy. The residents interacted with the animals by bottle-feeding young lambs, nursing chickens, patting my sheepdog, and yes, those screaming piglets were always a hit. This special therapy stimulated the elderly residents by giving them respite from the otherwise mundane and often lonely environment.

My unusual visitors were so stimulating, they often awoke long-forgotten memories, resulting in the residents reminiscing about the past with enthusiasm and excitement. This awakening was often dramatic, ending months of silence and depression, and consequently, the staff and I were often moved to tears. Over the years, I was privileged to listen to hundreds of stories as residents reflected on the lives they had lived. And I can say—without exception—no resident ever expressed a desire to have worked harder or longer. Anecdotes may have included work's interesting and amusing aspects, but most reflections featured family, hobbies, locations, and many "back in my day" comparisons.

Therefore, before we start mind mapping, I would ask that you consider how your older self will look back at work. Consider a few examples:

- George Lucas, who made over $3 billion from his Star Wars franchise and to this day still produces movies—a Hollywood icon.

- Melissa Caddick, a financial investment advisor in Sydney who allegedly misappropriated $30 million in client funds before disappearing. Her decomposed foot washed up on a beach months later—a scoundrel.

- Peter Brock, who was crowned *King of the Mountain* and a member of the V8 Supercars Hall of Fame for winning Australia's Bathurst 1000 endurance motor car race and Sandown nine times each—a legend.

- Chris Walter, Ansett Australia's youngest Flight Captain, who continued as Flight and Check Captain with other airlines long after Ansett's collapse, until retiring in his sixties—a career pilot.

- Rob McNeil, who began work as a carpenter but soon changed his vocation by joining NSW Fire and Rescue. He had a thirty-plus-year career that included leading Australia's response to Japan's 2011 tsunami disaster and being promoted to Assistant Commissioner—a strong leader.

- Jason Tydeman, who worked as a shoe repairer for over thirty-five years to pay off the modest home that provides security for not only his wife and children but also their children and his aging mother-in-law—a true provider.

How will you look back on your working career? A Hollywood icon, a scoundrel, a legend, a career pilot, a strong leader, and a true provider—all identities forged from years of work. In fact, there are more job descriptions than letters in this book, and probably just as many identities that have been attached to those roles. Therefore, you must choose the work you do wisely. It can become your identity—but not always.

For some, work is simply a means of paying the bills. Their identity will come from elsewhere: a hobby, a duty, an ailment, a relationship, an act of courage, an event, a belief, or even an opinion.

Therefore, the first question that needs to be answered through mind mapping work is, "What role does work play in my life?" This simple question may not always seem possible to answer, yet gaining clarity as to the role work plays in your life is critical in removing any distractions.

Let me explain. It is totally okay if work is simply a means to pay the bills. For millions, this is no doubt true. Money comes in, the bills are paid, and generally, you spend time with your friends and family, play sports, or focus on a million different types of interests. In this case, the role of work is simply to bring money into your life, nothing more. Those people may have many different jobs in life or just one. But it's always only a job to bring in the money; it's not their identity. Or, in addition to paying the bills, the money might be funding a particular interest, maybe even a magnificent obsession.

It's always interesting to hear the names of the young men that climb on the back of bulls at a rodeo. Electricians, carpenters, ranchers, concreters—all wanting to be known as a bull rider. The role of their work is to fund their dream; it's not their identity. Maybe that dream gains momentum and the bull rider starts winning prize money and goes professional. Then, work is not just work; it's his identity, just like the movie producer, artist, and rock star. This is where the magic happens because they are doing something they love anyway but getting paid for it.

What if work, however, takes up so much of your focus that other foundations suffer? The accountant who never stops working, the corner store owner who never seems to leave the shop, or the business owner who visits schools and parties with his menagerie of farm animals seven days a week. The role of work in these cases may be many things, but one role for certain is that of being a distraction. Distraction from what, you may be asking.

While work can be a powerful motivator as a means of wealth and self-identification, it can also be a distraction from living an abundant life. When you're earning a fortune but your mental health is failing—that's not living an abundant life. When you have fame but cannot keep a relationship with your husband or wife—that's not living an abundant life. When you are simply working your tail off while dreams and goals are ignored or forgotten, lost in a busy life—that's not living an abundant life. Finally, when you get to the end of your life and feel the regret of not having lived it better because you were distracted by work—that's not living an abundant life.

Now is your time to pause for a moment and ask what role work is playing in your life. Consider the consequences. Work can cause people to throw themselves off buildings and under trains; have heart attacks or mental breakdowns; lose friends, family, or marriages; become ill or unfit; take up gambling or drinking; and become depressed.

Fortunately, work can also be the elixir of life. Work can give happiness, freedom, wealth, health, and opportunity. It can define who you are and what you stand for. It can coexist with family, friends, and everyone in your life.

Creating a mind map will help identify this.

From your central foundation of work, branch out all the roles that you would like work to play in your new abundant life. For me this included the role of paying the bills, being flexible with hours worked, being able to work remotely, including some outdoor work, increasing my income to pay off my debts, funding other goals and magnificent obsessions, and for some—but not all—of my identity, and so on.

Once you have mapped out the role work will play in your abundant life, create a new branch from your central shape to mind map all your options for work, including all the pros and cons of each. If your current work is going to meet the required roles, brainstorm ways of improving this.

For me, as will be the case with most readers, it's rather complicated and even messy. I had a successful business that no longer played the desired role in my life. I first mind mapped my options: Franchise it? Increase my management team and step back? Find a partner? Sell it outright? I then broke each of those options down until I gained clarity on all my options.

As you can see from figure 7.6, I could indeed gain clarity on my options. However, the process of making decisions required research. For example, the option of franchising was appealing, so I met with a franchising expert who gave me income projections, timelines, and requirements to both set up the franchise structure and then continue as a head franchisor. As I said earlier, I placed all my cards on the table.

But once all the cards were on the table, how would I find the aces? Anyone who works in business can increase profits greatly with the 80/20 principle. However, this chapter is not a critique of business management and practice. There are many other books that will do that better. This is simply an overview of how I worked through the process to live a new abundant life—crossing that line in the sand by changing my work-related identity,

Figure 7.6: Mind map for work

reducing debt, increasing income, reducing work time, having flexible work hours, and so on. All those factors positively affected my happiness, health, community, and work.

It's also an example of someone trapped in a small business. In all Western countries, small businesses are (more likely than not) run by an owner-operator, arguably the most demanding business role of all, requiring multiple skills, long hours, lower ROE, and fewer benefits such as superannuation (defined-contribution plans) and workers' compensation. It's a role where the boundaries between personal and work life are vague at best and always demanding. According to the Australian Small Business and Family Enterprise Ombudsman, in Australia there are 2,506,000 small businesses that employ under twenty staff and only 2,533 large ones that employ over two hundred staff.[12] In the United States, there are 33.2 million small businesses.[13] Therefore, we should never understate the impact an out-of-balance business has on families and society as a whole. This makes my small business model relevant because there may be millions of business owners that feel trapped and need a wake-up call to break free from the business that now controls them.

After mind mapping and applying the 80/20 principle, I could now clearly see that if I restructured my activity to focus on the vital few (one of my smaller businesses that had a significantly better return on effort), the potential to increase profit was extremely high. Importantly, most of the roles I desired from work would also be achieved.

For many years, I had distracted myself from focusing on what would be one of the largest and most important decisions in my life. I got lost in the busyness of family, work, responsibilities, and a never-ending to-do list. As a direct result of my strategy of waking up early to focus on my life and after close to twenty years of hard work, my main business—the 80 percent—was sold. In practice, the process continued to be fully implemented over a few

12 Australian Small Business and Family Enterprise Ombudsman, "Contribution to Australian Business Numbers," accessed June 2, 2023, https://www.asbfeo.gov.au/contribution-australian-business-numbers.

13 Elise Boskamp, "40 Stand-Out Small Business Statistics," Zippia, February 9, 2023, https://www.zippia.com/advice/small-business-statistics.

more years as two other businesses were also removed from my mind, allowing me to focus on the vital few, unencumbered by the trivial many.

From my experience, we can bring about massive shifts in our lives by pausing and taking stock of how we spend most of our life—work. This is highly beneficial as it improves all other foundations of your life, activating goals that accumulate over a lifetime.

Whether you're self-employed, traditionally employed, a manager, an entrepreneur, part-time, an apprentice, about to retire, or even unemployed, you can always focus on the vital few. If an option feels out of reach or too unreal, use sub-branches and map what is necessary to requalify, reeducate, or retrain. What vital few will best qualify you for a new skill? What vital few are most productive? What are the vital few most profitable opportunities? And what vital few decisions are the most rewarding?

Decide how your work is going to fit into your life instead of life fitting into work, and expect the role work plays in an abundant life to evolve over time. What was once a means to pay the bills may change into a career with identity. A hobby may develop into a new career, a new identity, up to retirement. Or, like me, you may never want to fully retire. After all, why retire from doing something you love?

THE FIRST DAY OF YOUR NEW JOB

Many of my friends often make light of my work as part-time or semiretired because they see how my life has changed so dramatically over the past few years. In truth, those assumptions used to annoy me greatly, and I would always feel the need to defend myself based on the ghosts of the ingrained conditioning that I needed to be constantly busy, overworked, and under-the-pump to be worthy. As I write earlier, we wear being busy like a medal of honor, proudly displaying our exhaustion, all so we feel valued.

There is, however, some truth to their words. My business model has had a dramatic upgrade since embarking on my 5 AM experiment all those years ago. So it's true that I don't need to spend as much time actively working on it. But I still work extremely hard, only now I have a new job for a new company—and it's probably not the one most people think of.

I believe that no matter what work means to you, *mentally incorporating* your new abundant life is one of the best decisions you can make. By this, I mean truly believing yourself to be the owner-operator of a private, incorporated company called [Your Name] Incorporated (Bryce J. Chapman Inc., in my case). In this company, my job is president, and I have a fiduciary responsibility to the shareholder—me. Therefore, I am obligated to protect the company's primary objective, which is *to live a life of abundance*. The five departments I'm in charge of are:

- Department of Health and Fitness

- Department of Happiness

- Department of Family and Friends

- Department of Wealth

- Department of Work

All divisions must collaborate if the primary objective is to be successfully achieved. When my buddies comment that I'm not at work, they don't understand that I actually am—it's just that I'm now working very hard with focus at Bryce J. Chapman Inc.

Those deeply ingrained beliefs that we must incessantly toil—stay busy at being busy—must change. Becoming the president of your own incorporated company and taking charge of all five divisions will help you achieve that change.

This is the most important job you will ever have.

The advantage of being a 5 AMer is you can now make *this* job your priority. All the decisions, goals, early mornings, and focused attention now have a singular purpose—to live a new abundant life. At certain times, different departments will require closer focus, and it may seem that life is out of balance, because it is. But that imbalance is only short-term because when the president's in charge with a long-term view, all divisions return to balance.

There will be times when the department of work requires more focus, or the department of health and fitness, or family and friends, and so on. That's part of the strategy—life is never perfectly in balance!

Please accept this position with certainty. You have been given the job of president because no one else on the entire planet knows you as well as you do. And this courageous, exciting, adventurous, exhilarating, wondrous job is what will make your life outstanding.

—

So now, as president, you are in full control. It is up to you and no one else. The challenges you have decided to step up to are clear, and now is the time to take action, which is not only critical but is also the fourth goal activator, outlined in the following chapter.

CHAPTER 8

ACTION: THE FOURTH GOAL ACTIVATOR

You don't have to be great to start, but you have to start to be great.

—Attributed to Zig Ziglar

You've come a long way since first thinking about becoming an early riser. But by now, you understand that the practice of waking at this early hour is a metaphor for stepping up to successfully achieve your goals and magnificent obsessions. With a little work, you can bring your new abundant life into focus.

By taking action—the fourth goal activator—you will become the hero in your own life story, the bold one who takes that leap off the cliff into the distant waters below. Taking a leap into the unknown takes guts, but now you know what needs to be done and how you are going to do it. Yet, even so, how many times in your life have you had the knowledge but didn't take action? Without action, your goals will remain a plan—or even just a dream. In this chapter, we explore the concept of action and learn about two tools. The first helps you kick-start action on demand, so it takes off like a tornado. The second tool starts that energy every morning and keeps it on the correct path so you can successfully achieve your magnificent obsession and live a new life of abundance.

ACTION IS MOVEMENT

Although we talk about developing the mindset and strategies required to overcome inevitable challenges and obstacles, at its core, this book helps you identify where you are now and where you want to be. In other words, it helps you move from one place to another by taking action.

It is common for us to *know* what needs to be done. But instead of doing, we wait grounded in the comfort of standing by until the "right moment." A moment when a busy life frees up, when we feel mentally and physically energized, when we feel empowered—someday. But our goals simply won't be met unless we step up and take action whether it's the "right moment" or not. They say knowledge is power, but in this case, action is. When practiced daily, action propels our dreams forward, creating a new abundant life.

But what is action? Action is when you stop thinking about it and just do it—no matter what "it" is. Action is when we direct our energy at something that needs doing, such as a goal, activity, or task. Action requires the physical movement of your body to shift from one place to another, move an object from one place to another, or direct someone else or many others to do the same. Action closes the gap between where you are now and where you want to be in the future. There is no meaning in life without action, as you see in the following chapter. The reasons you live are to *take action* toward living the best life imaginable, morning after morning, bite by bite, and goal by goal.

Accordingly, your first goal each day is to take action by stepping out of bed early enough that you have time to work toward the second goal of the day, whatever moves you one step closer toward the achievement of your ultimate goal or magnificent obsession—the one you've broken down into achievable bites. When this is practiced repeatedly each morning, your mind adapts, making it easier, faster, and more productive. New habits are formed, goals are achieved, and your life of abundance is created.

Progressing through all the goal activators in this book, you can see that they not only contribute to the successful achievement of your goals but also do not act alone. They are attracted to each other, closely interlocked, and symbiotic. They exchange energy, force, and momentum, which completes a highly productive system that will keep moving forward once started. This physical movement is always a result of this chapter's goal activator: action. With any goal, targeted action relies on *discipline* to take each step. Action requires that each step is followed by another through *persistence*. Action will at some point be misdirected unless it's kept on target by *focusing* on what's important. And, as you also read in the next chapter, action fueled with *passion* results in the most extraordinary level of success.

THE ACTION-MOTIVATION VORTEX

How do we physically kick-start movement? More importantly, how do we take action that is intentionally directed toward the successful achievement of our goals *right now*?

To answer that, I reflected on my years of waking early to take specific action during that first hour or two of the day, and I observed the following outcomes:

1. *Any action leads to motivation.* When I lacked the motivation to achieve a goal—say, waking early to go to the gym or write this book—I simply stood up and took action, no matter what. The only thought in my mind was to *take action*, any action, no matter how small. Stand up. Wash my face. Have a drink of water. Dress and walk downstairs. By the time I was at my desk writing or on my way to the gym, I was in a motivated state. Even if motivation was delayed until I'd finished twenty laps in the rock pool, motivation always appeared. It never failed. Action always resulted in motivation.

2. *Motivation leads to intentional action.* When I naturally felt motivated or when motivation had been induced by action, I was then in a position to better channel energy into intentional and productive action. That is, I could start taking any action toward successfully achieving my goal, one bite at a time.

3. *Intentional action leads to higher motivation.* Now that I was taking intentional action toward successfully achieving a goal, a higher level

of motivation engulfed me. Now highly motivated, I could sit down and write for four straight hours, as if I was in a time warp. As I said—massive action!

In other words, action resulted in motivation. Motivation inspires more intentional action. That intentional action induces a higher level of motivation, and so on. This is a loop that increases in intensity as you rise with its energy and power. I call this the action-motivation vortex (AMV), and it not only kick-starts movement but also dramatically increases the energy and productivity of that movement (see figure 8.1).

Action creates motivation. Motivation creates action. So you can start the AMV from action, which leads to motivation, or from motivation, which leads to action. Either way, once started, they feed off one another and the vortex takes off, increasing in intensity and resulting in massive action.

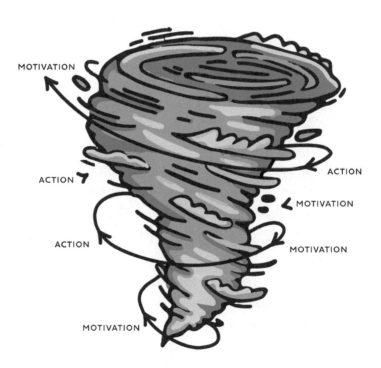

Figure 8.1: The action-motivation vortex

In other words, if you "just do it," the wheels get set in motion. You may find it helpful to give yourself the smallest task, such as "I will run for thirty seconds." If you run for thirty seconds, you'll find that it's easier to run for thirty more seconds than it is to stop—you have momentum now. Before you know it, you're running down the beach shouting to the moon! Your action *creates* motivation. (And I'm not joking. After I run, it's not uncommon to hear me shouting at the moon as I dive through the surf break before the sun rises.) I enjoy the run for fitness' sake but also because it *motivates* me. Ideas start flashing through my mind: concepts for my book, videos to shoot for my coaching, fresh creative ideas, and concepts so abundant and powerful that I'm not sure how to fit them all in. It's a flood of ideas, energy, and motivation. Suddenly, I have an extra spring to my step, a sense of certainty, and an overall increase in feelings of purpose and gratitude. The day is off and running, and I'm ready for action.

But even when action has started and you have stepped up to a challenge, it can still be difficult to keep taking the *right* action. As you know well by now, the busy life is always looming in the background, threatening to swallow, change, or eliminate goals without us realizing it. Before we know it, we are heading down the wrong path—again. Luckily, I developed a strategy for that.

THE MO STATEMENT: YOUR STATEMENT OF INTENT

To prevent the busy life from misdirecting goals, I developed what I call the MO statement, a tool that will protect and champion your dreams by guaranteeing that you continue taking massive and intentional action, day after day. Most importantly, this tool keeps the bull's-eye on your goal or magnificent obsession and directs all action on that target until the goal is finally achieved and victory is yours.

The MO statement helped me transform my life during some of its most critical periods of growth and change, and I know it can do the same for you. Its strength is derived from the concept of the magnificent obsession (MO)—a goal that has been elevated to the highest level of importance. MO also stands for modus operandi. *Modus operandi*, or "mode of operating," is a term used to describe someone's habitual way of working or their "method" of operation. For example, a burglar who targets a particular neighborhood, breaks in in a particular way, or even steals particular items has a telling MO. Therefore, it is helpful to connect this tool to your own modus operandi. Your MO statement is a document that clarifies and provides guidance for successfully achieving your magnificent obsession and your method of living a new abundant life. Smaller goals will also be achieved by focusing on the main event—the magnificent obsession, the MO—and creating opportunities for additional goals and dreams until you are successfully living an abundant life.

However, the MO statement includes one small caveat: you must set aside about ten intensely focused minutes each morning for it. Use this strategy when you need extraordinary help because it is extremely powerful. Given its time commitment, choosing when you use this strategy, and knowing its words and emotion have the power to change your life forever, can make all the difference in achieving success.

How to Write and Use an MO Statement

The MO statement involves writing out a one-page statement that focuses on your magnificent obsession and your new abundant life. Each morning, you take about ten minutes to rewrite this statement as your second goal of the day (your first goal being to wake up at 5 AM). This can be done every day or several times a week depending on the framework you have set. When you write this statement each morning, you stay focused on the target by keeping your magnificent obsession in plain sight and you eliminate the risk that a busy life will creep in and distract you. The MO statement allows you to confirm and reinforce what your main goal is every day, so it is always in your thoughts and given priority.

However, the MO statement is also highly adaptive. You do not always simply rewrite the same sentence over and over. Reaching a goal requires you to change and adjust your tasks and focus as you encounter roadblocks and hit milestones. When you carefully consider your words and how they direct your focus, the changes you make to your MO statement keep you on the correct and updated path. Think of the MO statement as an organic, ever-evolving declaration that changes over time because of daily reflection. As each objective is achieved, you replace it with a new one; as new information and new opportunities come to light, you'll update the statement. Tasks will be reprioritized and direction will change as you focus intensely on where you are now, where you want to go, and where you are directing your energy. This is not just an exercise in writing, reading, or thinking (like a daily affirmation). It's a repetitive and focused exercise in intentionally navigating your way toward success.

Consider a pilot flying a jet from Sydney to Los Angeles, which takes about fourteen hours. Even though the pilot knows where his destination is located and is taking action by flying the airplane, he must still check his instruments regularly to make sure his ever-diverging flight path is constantly bought back on course. Even though he doesn't need to spend the entire flight checking his instruments, a regular update is essential, as even a minor unchecked distraction from his desired path may result in a tragic accident. Your MO statement is your navigational instrument panel, allowing you to regularly check your own navigational instruments. It's far too easy for distractions to knock you off course, resulting in misdirection, inaction, procrastination, and abandonment of your goals.

When you work toward specific milestones—a smaller goal that is part of a larger goal or a step toward achieving your magnificent obsession—you become aware of your direction, the time necessary to get there, and what you are doing now to achieve success. Often, as your objective evolves, it becomes apparent you may now be on the wrong path. Sometimes you don't see this immediately, yet you will now see it sooner through this daily check, instead of being blinded by distraction in a busy life, day after day and year after year. The strength of your MO statement is its ability to intentionally navigate with a clear vision so you can adapt to your current circumstances.

As you advance toward your destination, don't be surprised if your MO statement changes significantly. I had been writing one of my objectives for many months only to delete it. This is not a failing of the MO statement or my actions—it's a major advantage. The regular action of writing out your MO statement prevents you from living an accidental life because it keeps your actions intentional and in constant reference to the bigger picture: your magnificent obsession (living an abundant life).

The action of writing the MO statement engages all five goal activators: discipline, persistence, focus, action, and passion. Further, it triggers the action-motivation vortex—resulting in massive action. That momentum continues into the other tasks that follow throughout the day. This tool is also a practice of daily gratitude. When you are aware of the successful actions (however small) you have taken toward achieving your magnificent obsession, you will be grateful for the small wins along the way. Having concrete, written evidence of your progress can increase feelings of self-worth, confidence, and motivation.

The MO statement involves repetitive thoughts in the quiet of the morning before distractions are present. This places you in the best environment to promote beneficial changes to how you think. Remember, neuroplasticity is best stimulated when neurons fire together along a path that is clear and focused. Writing your MO statement early in the morning promotes this because you are free from the distractions of noise, interruptions, commitments, and a busy mind. This is your time to be specific in the neural pathway you are practicing—better fitness, better health, better wealth, better happiness, and more. These are the pathways you must deeply entrench in your mind from your MO statement. This is what then becomes your modus operandi.

The time commitment—about ten minutes—may not sound like much. However, in practice, it may feel burdensome over time as your motivation moves from the ten minutes of writing your MO statement to a strong desire to simply dive in each morning and take action toward your goals. In other words, you may get the urge to skip writing to go running or take whatever other action. If this happens, check and adjust your framework as to when and how often you intend to write your MO statement. You may decide to write it every day during especially challenging periods when extremely focused action is required. Or you might dial it back to once a week or even once a month when your course is more certain and good progress is being made. From my own experience over the years, several times I have stopped writing out my MO statement, thinking it too time-consuming when all I wanted to do was start taking action each morning. However, this often resulted in lower motivation toward my magnificent obsession because it was not refreshed and refocused on with intention each morning. I lost energy.

A person's modus operandi is a telling indication of character, so it's appropriate as we seek a better life—a new life of abundance—to develop an MO statement that outlines both our magnificent obsession and our method. The following five steps will help you create yours. I offer some templates to get you started, as well as notes from my own MO statement that was written over a period of a few years during that critical time when I was deciding on my business and life direction. (They have been slightly edited to best guide you through the strategy.) One final note: everything you write in your MO statement must elicit emotion to anchor passion, which we discuss in more detail in the next chapter. For now, start with the action of writing out the first draft of your MO statement because every morning you can update it, making it better, more emotional, and more passionate.

Step 1: Decide on a Deadline for Your Magnificent Obsession

Remember, a goal is a dream with a deadline. And a magnificent obsession is a goal that is mandatory. You may already have a deadline in mind, but if you don't, set one now. And don't overthink it. A deadline can even be the start date. However, in your MO statement, it will more likely be a realistic end date of when you will successfully achieve a goal—remembering that it too can always be changed. Whatever your case is, set a deadline and then pair it with your magnificent obsession in a short sentence or two using the following template:

By [date] I have [your magnificent obsession description].
This results in [one or two outcomes].

This clear and concise opening paragraph gives you a sharp reminder of the critical target, opening with a date, invoking the urgency from a time limit, and providing a description of your magnificent obsession with one or two outcomes. The key here is writing it as though it has already been achieved. Here is my example from January 2009:

> By the end of March 2009, I have a clear direction for Kindifarm. This results in the payment of $XX in 2010, reducing debt and giving me financial freedom.

This opening paragraph helped free me from the distractions of my busy day to focus on one outcome—to finally make a decision about what direction to take my business. More importantly for me, this would result in finally having clear direction in my life as well as significant financial rewards.

At that time, making that single decision was my goal, which may appear uncomplicated. But having read my accidental life journal, you will appreciate that it was not. For me, it was a critical decision that I had been avoiding for many years. But after writing that paragraph, it was now a visible, concrete target. I had set a deadline that was achievable yet demanded focused action. I had also set an amount of money I wanted to receive that would reward me with financial freedom. I did not yet know the specific details of how that money would materialize, but the idea had been sparked—that was the important part for the time being.

Step 2: Outline What Needs to Be Done to Succeed

Clearly state the broad steps necessary to achieve that goal in a brief action plan, using your mind mapping from the previous chapter as your guide (if needed). You should have a pretty good idea of your plan from that. Remember, nothing is possible without action. What actions will you take? What are you prepared to do to achieve your magnificent obsession? Use the following template to get started:

> I will succeed by dedicating my 5 AM mornings to focusing on
> my magnificent obsession by [the specific tasks to complete it].

With this paragraph, focus only on the first two or three steps (goals) that you need to take to achieve a slightly bigger step (goal)—in other words, take small bites knowing that tomorrow's MO statement can move onto the next step (goal). Here is my example:

> I will succeed by dedicating my 5 AM mornings to focusing on
> my magnificent obsession by carrying out an extensive anal-
> ysis of my business options, including franchising, finding a
> partner, operating under management, selling, and any other
> option that may present itself.

For me, I knew the steps needed to make my business decision and find my direction in life. Notice that my first step was essentially research. I had to learn about my options before taking further action. Each morning, I would plan and organize the activity planned for the day, sometimes requiring me to reflect or even update my mind map. I would arrive to work early and highly motivated. During business hours, I attended meetings with franchising advisors, accountants, business brokers, and more. As each option was examined step by step, I got closer to achieving my magnificent obsession: deciding what direction I should take Kindifarm.

Step 3: Include All Foundations of Your New Abundant Life

Your magnificent obsession is part of living your new abundant life. This paragraph identifies your environment—where you live—and reinforces the strength of the life foundations you explore in chapter 7.

> My abundant life continues in [location] with [names]. My
> life is rich in happiness, family and friends, health and fitness,
> wealth, and work from an aware and focused mind.

Feel free to change, improve, or expand these foundational ideas to ignite your own passion and emotionally connect to your new abundant life. After all, living a new life of abundance is the greater purpose. Here is my example:

> My abundant life continues in Narrabeen and at the farm with Fiona and the kids. My life is rich in love, health and fitness, friends and family, happiness, wealth, and work from an aware and focused mind.

This paragraph allowed me to expand my focus beyond my business to my fitness—running on the beach under the moonlight (another life-changing decision). Later, I suggested to my surf club buddies that we start hitting the gym shortly after 5 AM.

Step 4: Craft Your Call to Action

The next sentence should acknowledge how your mindset and action are changing your life for the better. It's a call to action, an incarnation. This is not an affirmation—a statement that declares something to be true—it is more, much more. An incarnation is a living embodiment of your statement. You must feel, live, know, believe, be, and embrace every word with passion. Here's an example:

> My 5 AM habit is strong and well-established, resulting in success in whatever I choose to focus on this morning while working toward my magnificent obsession.

I continued to use the same wording outline in step 4 without change, as this paragraph is a short and sharp incarnation to start the day with the positive energy of a strong emotional jolt. It is important that I highlight the wording of this paragraph before we move onto the next step, as it is critical. I believe, with my hand on my heart, that whatever I decide to focus on and work hard toward each morning *will* result in success. These are not just words. For me, this is certainty in its literal meaning. And as I write them, it releases strong emotional energy that I physically and mentally feel, knowing that achieving success in that goal will come if I just keep taking action. Therefore, you must use content that will do the same to you, and believe it with your heart.

Step 5: Practice Gratitude through Performance Indicators

Now, list five performance indicators from yesterday's action that showcase your wins in progressing toward your magnificent obsession and living a new abundant life. This will help you practice gratitude. Try this template:

I am grateful for [one to five examples of gratitude].

Most cheer-worthy actions go past daily without acknowledgment, so each day feels like hard work—the grind of life! This paragraph is your time to enjoy life more by being grateful for the small wins and sometimes the big ones. When you do this regularly, the momentum of gratitude builds and life seems much better. After all, isn't that what living an abundant life is? Start living it now. Here's what I wrote:

I am grateful for

1. Waking up at 5 AM and getting to work at 5:30 AM.
2. An amazing meeting with a franchising expert—he loves my business.
3. Living in our family home so close to the beach at Narrabeen.
4. Having fun at the dinner table with the kids eating spaghetti bolognese.
5. Completing the advanced resuscitation first aid course at the surf club.

Some days are extremely productive, others are not. No matter, there is always something to celebrate. If gratitude is hard to find, make adjustments.

Tomorrow morning is a new day, a new start. To keep my overall magnificent obsession with a new abundant life fresh in mind, I list wins from various life foundations. After all, having dinner with my children at the table, talking, and enjoying each other's company is one of those little moments that we must be grateful for!

Putting It All Together

Having seen the MO statement broken down into its five steps, let's reconstruct it to show its conciseness. It only takes a few minutes to rewrite, but it's slightly longer when updates are required, as you will soon see. Here is my example from January 2009:

> By the end of March 2009, I have a clear direction for Kindifarm. This results in the payment of $XX in 2010, reducing debt and giving me financial freedom.
>
> I will succeed by dedicating my 5 AM mornings to focusing on my magnificent obsession by carrying out an extensive analysis of my business options, including franchising, finding a partner, operating under management, selling, and any other option that may present itself.
>
> My abundant life continues in Narrabeen and at the farm with Fiona and the kids. My life is rich in love, health and fitness, friends and family, happiness, wealth, and work from an aware and focused mind.
>
> My 5 AM habit is strong and well-established, resulting in success in whatever I choose to focus on this morning while working toward my magnificent obsession.
>
> I am grateful for
>
> **1.** Waking up at 5 AM and getting to work at 5:30 AM.
>
> **2.** An amazing meeting with a franchising expert—he loves my business.

3. Living in our family home so close to the beach at Narrabeen.

4. Having fun at the dinner table with the kids eating spaghetti bolognese.

5. Completing the advanced resuscitation first aid course at the surf club.

My goal to make that critical business decision was repeatedly activated each morning, refreshing my desire to achieve this goal, elevating its importance, and prompting me to make it the highest priority of the day. By doing this, the action-motivation vortex kicked in. I was highly motivated to take massive action. Four weeks ahead of my March deadline, the decision to sell the business I had started seventeen years earlier was made in a heartbeat. In a moment of certainty, I knew what needed to be done, and my life would never be the same again. From my experience, the biggest obstacles in life are often the decisions that need to be made. Therefore, the biggest goals we achieve are making those decisions. That is how we take massive action.

The simplicity of this strategy must never detract from its effectiveness in successfully achieving the goals highlighted in the statement. According to your progress, updates will be required, particularly to steps 1 and 2 because they highlight the goals to focus on and the action being taken for success, as the following updates show:

MO statement, March 3, 2009

By the end of March 2009, I will have Kindifarm on the market for sale. It is going to sell very well, resulting in a payment to me of $XX in 2009. This will pay off my debts, giving me financial freedom.

I will succeed by dedicating my 5 AM mornings to focusing on my magnificent obsession by carrying out an extensive analysis of my options for selling at the maximum price.

Again, taking massive action, I interviewed several business owners and talked to the accountant and other business advisors about the best way to sell the business. Within a week, it was on the market—again, well ahead of the deadline. I now had a sale price based on fresh information. Another update was required. As you can see, variations from the templates may occur during rewrites, and that is perfectly fine:

MO statement, March 11, 2009

By the end of September 2009, I will have sold Kindifarm for $XX. All aspects of Kindifarm are in great order, such as bookings, financials, staff, operational manuals, equipment, and farm infrastructure. The purchaser is extremely happy with the purchase, knowing it is one of Australia's most unique businesses. I have been paid fairly for starting up such a successful business and working hard for over seventeen years. The universe has delivered, bringing a balance to all my hard work and energy. I am a successful businessman.

This statement helped me focus on what I needed to do to prepare the business for sale, so it would be attractive to a great buyer. Over the months of rewriting my MO statement, I took massive action to bring all areas of the business up to the highest standard possible. The deadline of the end of September passed, but did that distract me? Not for a second. Every morning, I would rewrite my statement to keep my magnificent obsession alive. We kept operating as normal because we knew this unique business, the best in the country, would soon attract the best buyer. And it did. The discipline, persistence, focus, action, and passion had fully activated that goal, and it was achieved. On Christmas Eve 2009, an extremely motivated and appreciative buyer agreed to purchase the business for a sum that provided me with financial freedom.

On reflection, my MO statement was far from perfect, but that's its strength. The fact that I could easily update it and that it kept the most important elements in the front of my mind helped me maintain forward action during good times and bad, even when motivation wavered. Because I rewrote it most mornings, I could see my progress, even after a few months, which by any account is a successful outcome. I went from being out of control, overwhelmed, and burned out, owning a business that was void of direction, to selling it to a motivated owner who would give it new life, allowing me to move on to whatever future I then decided to focus on.

Now that the business had sold, I could focus on my next magnificent obsession. I switched the focus of my MO statement from the business to the first draft of this book. As you are reading it now, you already know that successful outcome.

Tips for an Effective MO Statement

While writing your own MO statement, the following tips will help you fine-tune it over time so you receive all the advantages this tool can offer.

PERFECTION IS THE ENEMY

Perfection is the enemy of progress, and no step in drafting the statement is the most important. Just write a first draft without judging it. Each day, you will read and revise the statement, which will get better and better as you progress. Yes, the overall details of your MO statement are important, but they are not carved in stone. Don't even worry right now if you think you have a very limited understanding of your magnificent obsession or even what living a new life of abundance is. Those details will evolve as you progress. The most important thing is to take action *now*. The aim of your statement is to activate movement, which then gains momentum.

Avoid analysis paralysis by completing each step with a broad understanding of the action required. Trust the process of the organic MO statement. Once action gains momentum, the full plan will reveal itself. Each step places you in a position closer to success. None are perfect or more important than each other.

CUSTOMIZE YOUR STATEMENT TEMPLATE

Customization is always key. Tools and strategies need to be flexible enough to work for you. If the MO statement template from this chapter feels limiting to you or like it is damping your creativity, change it. As long as the statement covers the following, you are good to go:

1. Decide on a deadline for your magnificent obsession

2. Outline what needs to be done to succeed

3. Include all foundations of your new abundant life

4. State your call to action

5. Practice gratitude through performance indicators

As long as the meaning of your statement's words achieves each of these five points, your customized MO statement will be just as powerful in helping you reach your goals successfully.

CONTROL YOURSELF, NOT OTHERS

Don't try to control another person, object, or situation with your statement's wording. If your MO statement is to win the lottery, forget it. Similarly, you are wasting time if your statement focuses on having your boss give you a promotion or having a client agree to a business contract. Those are wishes for the action of others, not your own actions. And you can't control the actions of others. If you want to *influence* others, focus on what you must do to attract or influence them to your way of thinking. Keep it all about you and the action you must take. For example, I didn't simply will someone to buy my business. I outlined what traits my business needed to make it highly attractive to a buyer, knowing that if I succeeded in this, then like bees to honey, a motivated buyer would see the opportunity.

Carefully craft your MO to keep it real—this is not magic or wishful thinking. It's a tool that keeps you focused and accountable.

HAVE INTEGRITY AND HONESTY

Set yourself up for success with your MO statement by aligning it with the principles of integrity and honesty. Your statement must uphold honor, truth, and honesty to yourself, others, and all things. Without integrity, dishonesty will creep in and attract dishonest people because it creates a sense of familiarity and comfort for them. Likewise, honesty will attract people who engage in honest behavior and are more likely to associate with others who share similar values.

For me, making my business attractive to a buyer meant each of those traits must be included with honesty and integrity. I knew without a doubt that my financial figures were truthful, my team was well trained and ready to work with a new owner, my operational manuals would far exceed any buyers' expectations, and all equipment and infrastructure was well designed and in great working condition. Furthermore, I believed—as I still do—it was one of Australia's most unique businesses. Had I been trying to pull the wool over buyers' eyes, it would have imploded and never crossed over the line.

Even if your MO statement doesn't involve other people, you must always be honest with yourself. If your statement is directing you down a path that does not sit well with you or your inner voice, correct it at once. Being dishonest with yourself in any way will always come unstuck in the long run, often with catastrophic results. Ask yourself, is this really what I want? Sometimes we lie to ourselves without knowing because we're distracted by a busy life.

MAKE IT A FAIR DEAL

If you're offering a service or selling products, be sure your MO statement describes your intentions so other parties have a fair deal, too. I'm not suggesting you discount, give away, or miss otherwise achievable and legitimate profits. I'm suggesting that you be fair to yourself and others—a win-win deal. However, the other party (because of inexperience, ignorance, or other reasons beyond your control) may still not fully recognize the benefits your opportunity offers. When this happens, the deal may fall over, but trust the process. The repetitive practice of writing and taking the correct action will eventually attract the correct buyer because you are offering a fair deal.

This far into the book, it should go without saying, but I'll say it anyway: any deal must be fair to ourselves as well, no matter the goal. We must protect self-love at all costs. For example, I would not set goals that required me to work fifteen-hour days, take on unhealthy routines, or set expectations so high they would be impossible to achieve.

Remember, it's also the journey, not just the destination that counts. And although we must work hard toward any goal, self-sacrifice over the long term is self-sabotage. Love yourself, and make the journey not only fair to yourself but an adventure you'll jump out of bed each morning to take part of.

MAKE YOUR DECLARATION TO THE WORLD INSPIRATIONAL

Stagnation is the killer of dreams—the opposite of action. By waking at 5 AM, you are making clear decisions with conviction and then stepping up to take action. Your MO statement is a declaration of that conviction to the world.

You may have been lost, or you may have spent years thinking about what you want to do or be. But you have decided to start becoming that person now, so proudly declare it to the world! Go ahead and step up on the soapbox to shout out: "Look out world! I have stepped up to take massive action by [insert your MO statement]."

For me, step 4 (your call to action) is my shout to the world.

So how can your statement incite a burning desire, inspiration, and emotion until you believe with certainty that the object of your desire—your MO—is yours? The world may never directly hear your declaration, but it will see the results. That I know with certainty.

TAKE IMMEDIATE ACTION

It is essential that you take action directly after writing your MO statement with any productive movement. Take a look at the actions you've listed in the statement and get to work on one of them, even if the action is small. It's still a step, and that step will lead to another. Taking action each morning then becomes your modus operandi. Your modus operandi is how you will achieve your goals and reach your magnificent obsession.

That window of opportunity to take action before the world wakes up is your time to start your momentum—the action-motivation vortex—that will carry you through the rest of your day, helping you achieve even more tasks and goals. Take guidance from your MO statement. Go for a run, start writing, start learning, start exercising, start working on getting that promotion, start developing that business idea, or start getting to work before your colleagues. Start doing whatever you need to do to live your new abundant life right now, and your magnificent obsession will also be successfully achieved.

—

So now you are all revved up to go, taking massive action like a person obsessed, but how do you keep the fire burning? What fuel will you use to drive all those goals over a long and prosperous life, all the way to the finish line? The fuel is *passion*—which is the fifth goal activator.

CHAPTER 9

PASSION: THE FIFTH GOAL ACTIVATOR

*Passion is energy. Feel the power that comes from
focusing on what excites you.*

—Attributed to Oprah Winfrey

Through the 5 AM Advantage, you see how the ten rules of discipline are used to motivate us to persistently take action toward achieving specific goals, which are now in focus without distractions. Further, you see that each small action you take, each step or goal you accomplish, or each bite you swallow accumulates over time into what we call progress. Progress moves you closer to achieving your magnificent obsessions and improving all the foundations of life so that a new abundant life can be lived.

But what ignites this desire to live a better life in the first place? And what fuels the motivation to be disciplined to persist for so long? The answer is passion—the fifth and final goal activator. When our passion is ignited, we can change the world.

In this chapter, we explore what passion is and how we can harness its power to activate our goals and live life as best we can, never settling for less.

I have always been a passionate person. I feel alive when passion naturally pulses through me or when, at times, I flick that switch on. I feel amplified, energized, in the zone, confident, and ready to take on any challenge. Passion gives me joy. I am thankful that our capacity for imagination, self-awareness, and introspection allows for such a deep expression of passion, one that goes beyond simple instincts and other emotional drivers.

That day with the screaming piglet was no doubt emotional. However, the feelings of anger, frustration, and overwhelm were soon surpassed by an explosion of passion when I thought about finally seizing control of my life. It was passion that moved me to draw that line in the sand. It was passion that moved me to start jogging on the beach under the moonlight. It was passion that moved me to tears when I listened to a good song or watched a good movie.

However, when passion is uncontrolled, it can become too intense, overwhelming other emotions and leading to impulsive and often destructive behavior. We've all heard of a crime of passion! As 5 AMers, thankfully, we will learn how to harness passion and always use it as a positive driver.

PASSION AND THE SYNERGY OF ALL FIVE GOAL ACTIVATORS

Let's start by taking a closer look at how passion adds to the synergy of all five goal activators. That way, we can best use passion to activate our goals, successfully achieve a better life, and help those around us live a better one as well.

We now know that discipline provides structure. Think back to the ten rules. This structure helps us practice the skill we'll need to take action, even when other people, our environment, or anything else tempts us to go off track. We also know that persistence is what helps us take action over the long term and step back to see the big picture of our progress even when setbacks occur. Focus keeps our eyes on the prize of our magnificent obsession—and the steps required to achieve it. But nothing will ever advance beyond the dream unless we take action initiated by motivation.

Importantly, as set out in chapter 2, all five goal activators do not work alone and gain their power through synergy with each other. However, the activator that is the rocket fuel to blast you to the stars is passion.

Passion is a strong emotional feeling of intense excitement and connection to something, which can drive us to pursue goals with greater enthusiasm and commitment. Passion can serve as a powerful source of intense motivation, providing a sense of purpose, inspiration, meaning, and direction that can help us stay disciplined, persistent, and focused in our active pursuit of a new abundant life.

When passion is added to life, it creates a powerful force for successfully achieving goals. When we become passionate about doing something (like riding a horse across the outback), we become highly motivated and disciplined to do whatever it takes. Our *why* runs deeper.

Discipline, persistence, focus, and motivation are mutually dependent and reinforcing, but when passion is added, it takes things to a higher level. And that is what I have been switching on as a 5 AMer—my daily practice of intentionally triggering passion. When that alarm goes off, passion is unleashed, giving me purpose and energy to wake up, step up, and successfully achieve not only the goal of waking early but other goals that follow in the day. Passion is nature's way of telling me something is important, so it can dominate my thoughts and action. And I know it will do the same for you.

PASSION ON DEMAND

Passion is naturally felt when we engage in an activity or pursuit that we intrinsically find rewarding and fulfilling. For me, I feel passionate catching the glimpse of the red or orange colors of a sunrise as I swim eastward down the length of the ocean rock pool. With each lap, the sun slowly rises, and I become intensely aware of the changing silhouette until my swim is complete. Every time I take in that special moment, I feel genuine gratitude. I feel a sense of joy, enthusiasm, and freedom that comes from being fully immersed in doing something I love. Something that aligns with my values and interests. Even when it's a challenge.

Passion can be experienced both loudly and quietly. Loud passion often explodes into expressions of energy, excitement, and action—such as when I shout out loudly under the moon when diving through a wave on a cold winter morning. In the world of the rich and famous, motivational speakers, and highly paid influencers, loud passion may seem to be what is required to be considered a passionate person. However, quiet passion is just as powerful and equally abundant, if not more so.

I am quietly passionate when I'm deeply moved by the panorama of our farm, the beach, the outback, snow-capped mountains, the image of my wife sleeping next to me, my children, a song, or a movie. In those moments, I don't need to scream out to the world. It's very personal—I'm in reflection with my inner self. While quiet passion may be merely a thought, it makes you ponder that thought at a deeper level, triggering gratitude, love, desire, happiness, and action. From my experience, passion often transitions between being either loud or quiet and even becomes a combination of the two. While swimming down the rock pool, I experience quiet passion—stroke after stroke—but when I finish my laps and look up at the sunrise, loud passion is unleashed to explode outwards in a shout and laugh.

If you're worried that you don't express your passion loudly, don't be. I love quiet passion. It's powerful. It's what drives me to pull the blanket off and get out of bed in the morning. I don't jump up fist pumping while loudly shouting out, "Yes!" I passionately think about my why and what I'm about to do—quietly.

Yet we often find ourselves thinking or doing something that we are simply not passionate about—maybe even one of the goals you want to achieve that you mapped out earlier. You may even be starting to recognize a pattern in your life of not being passionate about much at all. We are all unique, and the reason for an apparent lack of passion will vary from person to person. In some cases, it may be the symptom of an underlying mental health condition such as depression. But also, some of us simply don't place a high value on passion, being content with living a more routine and predictable lifestyle. No matter what level of passion you experience, this chapter helps you become more passionate than you otherwise would be.

If you're reading this book, however, I would guess you're not content with living an unremarkable and mundane life. Furthermore, I would guess you're passionate about making a change by achieving goals that are going to make your life better. I'm also sure, as you're reading a book about early rising, that you agree the character of a 5 AMer includes a passion for waking up early each day to live a better life. After all, a 5 AMer appreciates that by seizing the morning, they seize the entire day—ultimately seizing their life. I believe having a deep commitment to achieving dreams, goals, and magnificent obsessions is evident in the action of waking up early, and the thought of success stirs up passion from within. It fuels motivation and is so combustible that, once it's ignited, nothing will stand in your way until the focus of that passion is successfully achieved.

But I can also guess that for many of you, the idea of waking up at 5 AM doesn't ignite your passion. It may interest you so you are motivated, but the passion that would take this strategy to a higher level is still lacking. Thankfully, as I allude to earlier, passion can also be intentionally ignited so those feelings of euphoria intensify your experience. This is when the magic happens, even energizing otherwise day-to-day thoughts and mundane tasks. The fifth goal activator, passion, strategically bookends the four preceding goal activators—discipline, persistence, focus, and action—because when they are each infused with passion, they can all be taken to a higher level. And that's when life truly becomes outstanding.

So let's learn how to take advantage of naturally occurring passion, and then we can practice igniting passion on demand. At that point, goals are fully activated, and you have given yourself the best chance of success. You have taken responsibility for the things in your life you can control, and your accidental life will be a thing of the past—left behind the line.

The following strategy will harness natural passion to take things to the next level and ignite latent passion that you didn't know was there. You are prepared for this step because most of what you need is covered in earlier chapters. Now, you're just awaiting this final component of the strategy.

THE STRATEGY OF IGNITING PASSION ON DEMAND

Step 1: Set Clear and Meaningful Challenges

Igniting passion on demand requires us to intentionally take our experiences up to the next level, starting in this first step of fine-tuning the framework of our goal that we learn in rule 4 and exaggerating what it means to us from rules 1 through 3 (think it, own it, and know your why). But critically, we must always think and act as if our goal is a challenge, not a task, job, exercise, project, duty, or undertaking—all goals are challenges.

We intuitively step up to a challenge, and the neural networks that help us meet challenges start to fire. Additionally, when a higher meaning is attached to a challenge, passion kicks in to instinctively prepare you (both mentally and physically) for the battle ahead. That higher meaning needs to be way higher, so be prepared to stretch normal perceptions. In other words, exaggerate. By working on and succeeding in this challenge, you are a warrior, a pillar of unbeatable strength, a rock star, Hercules, an icon, or a legend. You are whatever you are striving to be—but bigger. Have that conversation with yourself, and remember your physicality. Stand tall; you're invincible.

Step 2: Anchor Passion

Even if passion is lacking, we have all been passionate about something in life at one time. Go back to those one or more moments and reactivate the feeling of passion—right now. Note how your body and mind are reacting: heartbeat, pulse, breath, posture, facial expression, physicality, and so on. While doing that, reflect on the reasons you feel passionate about that moment—your why. What does it mean to you, why is it moving you, when does it happen, and so on?

Now, while feeling and recognizing the reasons behind passion, anchor them to the task at hand or whatever you want to be passionate about. Envision yourself doing the task or completing the goal and imagine that your body is reacting with passion. Try to picture it so clearly that it invokes your emotions to the extent that you have an outburst of excitement, tear up, laugh, scream, or feel the hairs on your arms stand up—feel it. With practice, you can anchor those two or more moments together on demand.

Step 3: Find Additional Inspiration

Your goal should already excite and interest you, motivating you to work persistently toward its success over time. However, when motivation fades (as it often does), you can reignite your passion by finding additional inspiration. Today's technology makes this instantaneous. Inspirational music, podcasts, audiobooks, YouTube videos, and more are all ready and waiting on your phone or computer. Reading books, talking to people, attending events with inspiring speakers, immersion in landscape and nature, and generally surrounding yourself in an uplifting environment will all help get the blood pumping to ignite your passion. In other words, put yourself in an environment that ignites you, so you can carry that feeling forward into all you do.

Step 4: Regularly Play Full Out

Repetition when engaging in activities and playing full out will ignite passion. Playing full out means that you give something your complete and total effort, focus, and attention. It means doing everything in your power to achieve your challenge (goal) and taking action to the best of your ability without holding back or leaving anything on the table. When you play full out regularly, it becomes a mindset, a way to approach life. It eventually becomes hardwired into your neural network, and at that point, it's not something you strive to be but something that you are. And that can ignite the passion in your life you need to achieve your goals.

Step 5: Step Out of Your Comfort Zone

Passion thrives when you step out of your comfort zone, as it requires a high level of commitment, determination, courage, and guts. It means pushing yourself beyond your limits and taking risks to successfully achieve your goals. Stepping out of your comfort zone puts your mind into fight or flight mode, and all your senses become acute—we are all passionate about our own survival, whether we are aware of it or not. Stepping out of your comfort zone keeps things new and fresh, which ignites passion. Find ways of doing old things differently. Mix it up, up the ante, adopt new approaches, be bold, and embrace uncertainty.

Step 6: Focus on the Positive

Passion is a positive mindset because it is a strong feeling of enthusiasm, excitement, and dedication toward something we find meaningful, interesting, and important. Celebrate with abundant joy the small wins along the way. Go overboard with intense, lively, energetic, and self-congratulatory emotions—they will ignite passion. After all, you're living life as best you can. That's outstanding! Well done!

—

Any single one of these steps may be enough to ignite your passion. However, going through all six steps gives you the ability to evoke a strong emotional feeling of intense excitement and connection to something you decide needs passion where it is otherwise lacking.

To practice passion on demand, the remainder of this chapter takes you through the process of igniting passion in something I know many people are dispassionate about: waking up at 5 AM. Developing a passion to rise early is critical, as it helps you take your first action of the day and it will help imbue the rest of your morning (and day) with the motivation you need to do and be your best. If you can intentionally foster passion for this one action—waking up at 5 AM—you will know you can intentionally ignite passion in whatever else you want to do.

HOW TO BE PASSIONATE ABOUT
WAKING UP AT 5 AM

Without a doubt, over the years of talking about the strategies in this book, the waking up at 5 AM part has always been a deterrent. Many people believe they are not morning people and would never be able to or want to rise early. There is simply no way I could convince them that this strategy can change their life because, remember, a life change cannot be forced on anyone. Change must come from within, and you must be ready to have an open mind. You must be impartial enough to accept that even though you're not passionate now, there may be a chance you can become passionate about waking up at 5 AM through this process.

The good news is that, in my experience, all you need is a *little* interest in becoming a 5 AMer. That is enough to become a passionate 5 AMer.

I am a passionate 5 AMer. I wake up early most mornings. How have I continued to do so year after year, through the dark months of winter, during injury, periods of lost motivation, and good times and bad? First, I have already proven to myself that I can do it. And if I can do it once, I can do it again. If I did it yesterday, I can do it today. Second, I am passionate about waking up at 5 AM and truly believe it gives me the ultimate advantage. But how do I keep that passion burning?

We are now going to use the previous six steps to help you become passionate about waking up at 5 AM. I detail what that looks like for me in the context of waking up at 5 AM at a few specific periods of my life. Additionally, I prompt you to ask yourself several questions in each step, and I share answers from my own experience for guidance. I encourage you to not only take the time to reflect deeply in answering these questions but also take it to the next level by identifying any triggers that evoke emotion. When you do, you will become acutely aware of where passion is found—greatly increasing gratitude, love, and an appreciation of life—giving you access to the switch to turn on your passion for waking up at 5 AM.

Step 1: Set Clear and Meaningful Challenges

I use the word *challenge* many times in this book, and I do so with good reason. We *step up* to a challenge—we never *step down*. All challenges may appear out of reach at the start. Yet, with action and over time, we change and our reach is extended until we evolve and succeed.

You also know that I love to challenge myself, which is why this early-rising experiment appealed to me all those years ago. The challenge of waking at 5 AM to add adventure to my life sent me into a frenzy of excitement and enthusiasm. Self-improvement can take many forms, and after years of reading books, listening to CDs, and attending seminars, now it was time to try something new. The idea (goal) instantly felt like a challenge, and I was in—challenge accepted.

My why is to somehow improve myself and grow—to *change*. And when I think back to my reason for bungee jumping from the 365-foot-high Victoria Falls Bridge over the Zambezi River in Zimbabwe, it's no different. I'm not an adrenaline junky or risk taker; far from it. But I knew somehow that experience would make me a better person—and I believe in a small way that it did—it changed a fragment of my character.

Likewise, waking up early is a small fragment as I step up knowing I'm improving myself, growing, and changing. But to make that resolve a passion, gaining clarity of that challenge and its meaning is critical, so ask yourself these questions.

- What *specifically* is the framework of your challenge?

    From my experience, my challenge is to wake up enthusiastically as a 5 AMer. To ignite passion, I must take that up a level by gaining even more clarity of my framework, as outlined.

    o Monday 5:30 AM wake up. Walk over to the beach for a 6:00 AM surf swim before coffee at the club at 6:30 AM.

    o Tuesday 5:00 AM wake up. Walk to the club gym by 5:20 AM for a workout followed by a cooldown surf swim before coffee at 6:30 AM.

- Wednesday 5:00 AM wake up. Walk to the beach by 5:20 AM for a three- to five-mile run followed by a cooldown surf swim and coffee at 6:30 AM.

- Thursday 5:00 AM wake up. Walk to the club gym by 5:20 AM for a workout followed by a cooldown surf swim before coffee at 6:30 AM.

- Friday 5:00 AM wake up. Drive to the rock pool by 5:25 AM to swim two-thirds of a mile. Then coffee at 6:30 AM.

- Saturday 5:15 AM wake up. Drive to the rock pool by 5:40 AM for the same swim. Then coffee and hot breakfast at 6:30 AM.

- How can you define your challenge in greater detail?

  From my experience, using my swimming days as an example, these are the rules I must follow each morning.

  - I swim two-thirds of a mile (one kilometer), which is twenty laps.

  - I swim freestyle.

  - I must start before sunrise.

  - I never wear a wet suit. However, a rubber cap in winter is allowed.

  - There is no backing down, even if the waves make it rough, it's freezing cold, or it's pouring rain (unless it's too dangerous because of a storm and extremely large surf, which is rare).

  - I cannot stop for more than a few breaths at each end of the pool.

  - I must reach forward with each stroke to stretch my injured shoulder as best I can to help its flexibility.

  - I must maintain a positive attitude for each lap as I count them to twenty. Meaning, even on laps one through four, I cannot feel negative by thinking about how many more I still have to go.

- I must also take mental note of my mindset throughout the swim, acknowledging my thoughts for what they are. That awareness of thought puts me in a meditative state.

- Have you made allowances for variations in your framework?

  From my experience, yes, my framework makes allowances for when I'm away from the coast at the farm. Then, I may wake early to write, go for a horse ride, or simply enjoy a sunrise.

- What does your challenge really mean to you—your why (how will you connect it to emotion)?

  From my experience, after restructuring my business, I now have more time during the day to take action on several of my goals (such as completing this book) other than work. Therefore, the reasons I now wake up early are primarily health, fitness, and mind. My experience with diversional therapy in nursing homes, my back rehabilitation, and the bull accident allowed me to attach emotion to my goal of swimming in the rock pool, invoking passion for its successful outcome.

  It might surprise you, but I haven't always been passionate about swimming (for the sake of just swimming laps, anyway). Therefore, I must increase its meaning to ignite my passion, especially in the dark months of winter when my motivation is low. I do this in two ways. First, I intentionally elevate my *simple habit* of swimming with my surf club buddies to a *hard and fast tradition* of swimming with my surf club buddies. After all, we've been swimming together for more than a decade. To me, a tradition has more importance and weight to it than a habit. Breaking the tradition would mean dishonoring an unbreakable code among brothers. This means it must be continued under all circumstances (even the bull accident didn't keep me from swimming for too long). My buddies help me with this mindset. Each of us would berate a buddy who broke tradition, and we encourage each other to stick with it.

Second, I have placed increased significance on seeing the sunrise each morning when I swim. The sunrise already inspires me, so I just take it to the next level. I do this by emotionally overstating its significance, believing no one else on the entire planet is witnessing such an awe-inspiring sunrise as I am today. I am so lucky and grateful to see it, and swimming is the reason I get to.

Being this specific about the challenge (goal) and its meaning ignites passion. This is how we change our state of mind. Even while writing this, I feel a change in my state—increased heart rate, adrenaline, and anticipation. As I said earlier, it's magic.

So, what questions can you ask yourself that will take the rules of thinking it, owning it, knowing your why, and setting your framework to the next level? The questions are just the start, see what level you can take it to and experience how your passion ignites as a result.

Step 2: Anchor Passion

I believe I'm naturally a passionate person. I've had many passionate experiences and often think back on those times to tap into and harness those feelings when I need motivation. Over time, I have developed strong neural pathways that enable me to trigger those thoughts and emotions on demand. If you find this difficult, following the process outlined in this step will wire those pathways into strong networks. With practice, you can anchor those two or more moments together—on demand—to ignite passion. It might take time at first, but as you get better, it can happen in an instant.

That's the power of anchoring passion. All you have to do is find a memory that anchors you to passion. That way, you can incorporate it into your 5 AM routine to get you excited about waking up. Use the following questions to help you find your passion anchor. It's important you allow yourself to get carried away with acknowledging moments of passion, as I have done in my example answers. My catalog of passionate experiences could fill many pages, so I only include a selection here. Your moments of intense passion will be different than mine, and that's okay! So ask yourself the following questions.

- Is there any part of the early morning, such as a sunrise, that passionately moves you?

  From my experience, yes, I have a vast catalog of passionate memories associated with early mornings:

  o Riding my horse directly into the sun rising over the flat horizon of the open plains of Western NSW.

  o Witnessing first light over the snowcapped mountains of British Columbia, Canada, with a fresh bag of trees ready to be planted.

  o Smelling the fresh, crisp air and hearing the sound of awakening birds at daybreak while camping in a swag next to a creek, when mustering cattle in outback Queensland.

  o Watching the sun rising over the Mediterranean from a villa in the Greek Islands.

  o Seeing the sunrise over the ocean through the open door at the gym while at the same time curling dumbbells, thinking this is the best view from any gym in the world.

  o Admiring the silhouette of a boab tree at sunrise while horse trekking with my wife, daughter, and friends in the Kimberleys of outback Western Australia.

  o Sipping a cup of coffee alone as first light filters through a foggy daybreak at the farm.

- What other moments have you felt passion in life?

  From my experience, moments with my wife often ignite massive passion. It might just be looking at her beautiful face from a certain angle, how a dress fits the curves of her body, or a touch of skin in the night.

  Driving into our farm after being away for a week or two, looking out to the paddocks, seeing the cattle, calling in the horses, and watching them run up for a pat also ignites massive passion.

Even seemingly trivial moments with my children often ignite passion: talking over a coffee on the front porch, laughing together at the dinner table, watching *Pirates of the Caribbean* together for the umpteenth time, or simply noticing how content they are at home—happy, comfortable, and safe. It can be the little things that ignite massive passion. All those moments are priceless because I am passionate about them.

- How does thinking deeply about those moments feel? How is your body and mind reacting?

    From my experience, I easily feel enthusiasm, love, excitement, happiness, positivity, contentment, gratitude, certainty, intro-spective, and alive. I feel my heartbeat increase and the pulse in my neck becomes apparent. My breath deepens and I feel in tune with my surroundings, at one with nature, and in the moment. In the now. I may feel a lump in my throat or even a tear in my eye. If I'm with someone, I'm very expressive in language, relaying the emotions from within. In short, my passionate thoughts are extremely powerful.

- Reflect on the reasons you feel passionate about the moments you detailed earlier. What does it mean to you? Why is it moving you? When does it happen? And so on.

    From my experience riding my horse in the outback sunrise, it was knowing I was alive with enhanced senses! Breathing in the air, the sound of hooves on the ground, the snorting of nostrils, the smell of the horse's sweat, the fresh cool air, and the changing colors over the horizon. It was sensory overload.

    With my wife and children, it's love—an extremely powerful emotion—but also contentment, happiness, pride, wonder, and appreciation. Maybe I compare it to my childhood, which seemed to lack so much love after the devastation of my father's death. The thought of how good my life is now stirring deep passion.

- Can you practice reactivating the feeling of passion right now?

From my experience, I do so through visualization, which is creating a mental image that recalls memories of what I was seeing, hearing, feeling, smelling, tasting, or what I was thinking. And if I can visualize more than one of those, all the better.

- How can you practice connecting a known passion that you have previously experienced to a new challenge?

From my experience, when I encounter moments of passion, I make an intentional mental note about what I'm doing and how I'm feeling in that moment. I do this knowing that at some time in the future I will need to recall those feelings. As I have been doing this for many years now, when a new challenge presents itself, I can easily recall those feelings and connect them.

Again, use these questions as the starting point to take your experiences to the next level. One last tip that I find extremely helpful is to set my future challenges when in a state of passion. So, when I'm on a high after having finished twenty laps in the cold water, I acknowledge how great I feel at that moment (the passion) and make the decision—with certainty—to do it again. The next morning, I can recall those feelings of passion, accept that the decision to step up has already been made, and know with certainty that I am going to feel outstanding again when I achieve that challenge.

Step 3: Find Additional Inspiration

We live on a beautiful planet, abundant in inspirational sensory gifts—sights, smells, sounds, and more—that we share with amazing people whose words of wisdom or stirring speeches and music inspire us to live a better life. This abundance of marvelous encouragement can be overlooked and can dim as we struggle in a busy life full of demands, pressure, and unfair expectations. However, those times of strong resolve are easily reinvigorated with practice when you have identified what inspires you.

Have you ever been taken back to a long-forgotten memory by a smell, taste, sight, or maybe a song? It happens to me all the time. David Bowie's song "Heroes," without fail, takes me straight back to the day my mother, two sisters, and I drove across the outback in a small Ford Escort, in the sweltering heat of summer, to start a new life in Sydney after my father had passed. The song (being top of the charts back then) came across the crackly car radio with words and sounds that, for some unknown reason, moved me with such deep emotion. Now, every time I hear it, I'm instantly returned to that moment. I'm back over forty years ago, looking out of the open car window with the wind in my face. If I ever need to access passion, I can turn on that song.

With a little preparation, you can do the same—either first thing at 5 AM or by preparing your mindset the night before in anticipation of waking up. Additionally, you can ignite a deeper level of commitment to waking up at 5 AM by asking yourself the following questions.

- When have you felt energized and passionate while having a sensory experience, such as eating, watching videos, or listening to music?

  From my experience, some of my most memorable moments of feeling extremely passionate from music are when I'm driving. Australia is a land of vast open space, and I'm regularly in the car all day or at least for a few hours driving up to our farm. The right music can elevate my passion, making the journey not only enjoyable and seemingly faster but also highly creative. Fresh ideas about new or existing projects abundantly flash into new thoughts and are viewed with positivity, possibility, and high motivation. It is often a very intense and moving experience. I listen to music while jogging and writing. Regarding video content, I become most passionate when watching a good movie. However, I also find motivational content on YouTube can change my state in an instant.

- What can you do to prepare yourself so when you need motivation, that passionate content is instantly ready at hand in the morning?

From my experience, I have an old iPod Shuffle that has Tony Robbins's gratitude and priming tracks ready to go anytime. I particularly love this when jogging on the beach in the mornings and have been doing it for so long now that, within the first few seconds of listening, my passion has been ignited and I'm in an energized and focused state, happy to be alive so early in the day.

I also have a focus playlist on Spotify that I listen to while writing. To take this up a notch, I even have a short list of extra favorite albums such as Philip Glass's *Koyaanisqatsi*, which puts me into an intense state of extreme passion and activates a high level of creativity and productivity when I listen to it.

- What book have you read that has ignited your passion, and perhaps changed your life? What other books do you want to read?

  From my experience, I read most nights before turning out the light as part of my preparation for early rising. Reading an inspirational story helps me go to sleep with a positive mindset. Recently, I read *The Shepherd's Life* by James Rebanks, which stirred my passion, being an inspirational story of an intelligent man who decided to continue the family tradition of life on a farm in England. Reading this story, I appreciated the importance of protecting such a way of life in a changing world, I reflected on the life I have chosen to live, and I was inspired to stay my course of being closely connected to the land—my chosen path.

  Also, I always have an audio book downloaded and ready to listen to when I'm in the car. Those hours are gold for content intake, and on occasion, this can ignite passion when ideas are discussed that align with my goals.

- What public speaker gets your blood pumping? Can you book ahead for their next tour? Who else would you like to see?

  From my experience, I recently took my son to see Jordan Peterson talk in Sydney, which we both loved. Next, we are seeing Jocko Willink when he tours Australia. No matter who you see, inspiration to live a better life adds passion, making the challenge of waking early seem much more worthwhile.

- What program would you consider attending?

    From my experience, I have completed all of Tony Robbins's programs, starting with his iconic Unleash the Power Within (UPW), which includes an amazing fire walk—seriously, a passionate challenge to conquer. This type of additional inspiration might seem expensive. But one of my favorites, Business Mastery, was instrumental in reigniting my passion for business and greatly helped increase my profits—paying for all the programs many times over. Take time in researching what program is right for you; there are many that are worth spending both your time and money on if you truly want to ignite your passion. At this date, I have two future Tony Robbins seminars booked, which I'm attending as a leader.

- Where are you when you're inspired by your surroundings? How can you spend more time there?

    From my experience, I find an abundance of inspiration at the farm—a view over the paddocks with the cattle grazing, the horses, a sunrise, a sunset, the sound of the birds, and so much more. The farm is where I'm writing this section of the book. I also find passion at the beach, especially before sunrise—the smell of the salt air, the sound of the waves gently breaking on the beach, dolphins swimming in the still waters of first light, or the mountainous swell of a winter storm. Over the years, I have prioritized both where I live and where I spend most of my time, particularly work, to stay in line with what drives my passion.

Before moving on to step 4, access your passion right now by using one of your additional inspirations. Put your headphones on and listen to a song or some music, watch a motivational video on YouTube, or walk outside and immerse yourself in the environment. Make it simple and instantaneous—it's that easy.

Step 4: Regularly Play Full Out

Every time I have attended a seminar, whether live or virtual, the speaker asks that we play full out. It is obvious in that situation that they are asking us to listen acutely to everything said at the event, participate as best we can, and never hold back from becoming emotional, immersed, and totally committed to the process and strategies being outlined. It's always good advice because when you play full out—like you used to as a child—it ignites passion and everything becomes fun.

But in the real world, it can be more challenging to play full out with the challenge of waking up at 5 AM. To help, ask yourself the following questions, and see that playing full out when that alarm goes off can still be child's play.

- When have you ever played full out?

    From my experience, three of my children and I went skydiving a few years back. We all played full out, knowing we were experiencing something that we would remember for the rest of our lives.

- How did it feel knowing you had played full out?

    From my experience, it felt amazing to have shared such an awesome moment with my children. It was fun, and we were all thrilled and exhilarated from knowing we had jumped out of a perfectly good airplane at ten thousand feet. We shared how we found that experience afterward and, in doing so, got to understand each other on a deeper level. It was simply great fun. Even when I think about it now, passion is ignited.

- How can you learn from that experience to play full out more often in life?

    From my experience, there are many times now when I use this idea of playing full out to enhance an experience I'm about to have and ignite passion. I simply ask, *What do I need to do now to make this a ten-out-of-ten experience?* In other words, *How do I play full out?* I have recently had this conversation with myself before departing on a long and at times challenging journey, trekking on horseback in Western Australia's outback Kimberleys. I wanted this to be an amazing experience for not only myself but also everyone else on the ride. So, before we departed, I set my own standard and expectations of how I would act and behave for it to be a ten-out-of-ten experience. In doing this, when a situation arose that might result in me not playing full out, I could call myself out.

After driving three thousand miles across the country, the day before the start of the ride, I fractured my coccyx bone (at the base of my spine) while jumping into water incorrectly from a cliff into Lake Argyle in Western Australia. Obviously, riding a horse for a week was not ideal for such an injury. However, as I had had the "play full out" conversation with myself before departing, I didn't complain once about it. I may have joked a few mornings, asking, "Who put concrete on my saddle?" because the seat was so hard and uncomfortable with my badly bruised bottom, but I didn't complain in earnest. Doing so would not have helped, likely reducing the experience for myself and others on the trip.

My reward for playing full out—the ride was amazing. I dealt with the injury after the ride and the long drive home, and now I look back on that ride with passion, as does everyone else. Deciding to play full out ahead of an event is a powerful mindset to ignite passion. Try it when you really want to step up and passionately give something 100 percent.

- How can you play full out when waking at 5 AM?

  From my experience, when I make the decision to wake up at 5 AM, I always do my best to adhere to the rules of discipline and all five goal activators, including passion. By doing this, I know I'm giving it 100 percent and playing full out. In a nutshell, that looks like this:

  o Think it: I am a 5 AMer who is passionate about waking up early to start each day and live life as best I can.

- Own it: It's up to me and no one else to get out of bed and step up!

- Know your why: I'm going to prove to myself, my family, my friends, and my peers that I can live life the best way I know how and successfully achieve what challenges I step up to.

- Create a framework: As described in step 1, I know exactly what is required of me when I wake up.

- Be prepared: The night before, my bag is all packed and ready. I'm reading a great book before lights out at a reasonable time. I'm about to have a great sleep and an amazing morning awaits me. I love this life!

- Make a decision: The alarm goes off. This is the first decision of my day; I'll make it a good one!

- Apply pleasure and pain: When I get up, I'll feel energized, successful, and worthy, having achieved my morning challenge. If I don't get up, I'll have let my buddies down, but worse, let myself down. Ouch! That will hurt!

- Reward yourself: I'll reward myself extrinsically with a sunrise and coffee and intrinsically because I know I'm living life as well as I can, enjoying the banter and camaraderie with my buddies.

- Be flexible and reject perfection: There's no need to be flexible tomorrow morning, I'll be getting up as planned!

- Set yourself up for success: Everything I have physically and mentally prepared is helping me succeed not fail.

By playing full out, 100 percent every morning, I'm going to achieve my goal of waking at 5 AM to the very best of my ability; nothing will be held back. I have discipline, I'm focused, those actions are repeated persistently every morning, and my passion is lighting the way.

Make the decision right now that tomorrow morning you're going to play full out in the challenge of waking up early. In addition to applying the ten rules of discipline specifically to waking at 5 AM, ask yourself, what must I do to make tomorrow morning's experience a ten-out-of-ten experience? Accordingly, quickly set your mental framework for that to happen, and in the morning when that alarm goes off, awaken to your why and play full out!

Step 5: Step Out of Your Comfort Zone

Not everyone believes in change. In fact, they resist it. Often, I'll ask someone how they want to improve their life, and they tell me straight out, that everything's fine. Clearly, that is not always the case.

Pink Floyd's song "Comfortably Numb" was written as a warning. Being comfortably numb is a dangerous place to live. You have gotten used to the pain. The dream is lost. Life is coasting along on autopilot, and you're hiding out in the cocoon of your comfort zone, living an accidental life! When we live within our comfort zone, we know what to expect, there is little risk, and we always feel at ease. Life is rarely challenging, and there is no need to extend or stretch ourselves.

This step helps you clearly see that we often step out of our comfort zone, which results in many benefits. Additionally, your daily challenge of waking at 5 AM is also taking you out of your comfort zone. You will also learn to recognize when your practice is getting too comfortable so you can shake things up. Ask yourself the following questions.

- When have you lived too long in your comfort zone?
  From my experience, without knowing it at the time, avoiding the decision to change my business structure and sell Kindifarm was living too long in my comfort zone. Yes, I was burnt out and overwhelmed, far from comfortable as we might consider it. However, I was definitely comfortably numb—living too long avoiding the hard decisions.

- When have you stepped out of your comfort zone?

  From my experience, I've done this in going to college, jackarooing, starting a new job, leaving a job, traveling the world with
  a backpack, tree planting, swimming in the Arctic Ocean, starting
  a business, leading meetings, making decisions, buying a house,
  buying a farm, selling a business, attending courses and seminars,
  skydiving, white water rafting, horse riding, surfing, motorbike riding, scuba diving, jumping into water from cliffs, writing this book,
  waking up early, saying hello to someone new, and so on. So I step
  out of my comfort zone all the time, as I expect you do, too. But
  maybe you don't realize just how many times.

- When did you grow or learn a valuable lesson from stepping out of
  your comfort zone?

  From my experience, I grew or learned something every time I
  stepped out of my comfort zone. Every time. Stepping out of my
  comfort zone to change the direction of my life resulted in many benefits. But one previous experience I cherish was when I was driving in
  my ute (pickup truck) by myself, away from all my family and friends,
  to go jackarooing. Heading into the outback and working hard on a
  56,000-acre sheep and cattle property was definitely living out of my
  comfort zone. But the rewards were many. I reconnected to my love
  of the land, showed high work ethic, proved the ability to challenge
  myself, rode horses, worked livestock, serviced a tractor, castrated
  calves, and so on. It was the most influential experience of my life—all
  from stepping out of my comfort zone.

- Looking back at those moments of stepping out of your comfort
  zone, do you now feel the passion toward each activity or situation?

  From my experience, yes. When I read back through the list of
  times I have stepped out of my comfort zone, I feel passionate about
  them all. I must say that the level of passion runs a great deal deeper
  than the words written on this page. I am physically and emotionally moved simply by thinking about those moments. I feel proud,

courageous, inspirational, brave, strong, manly, and adventurous. Passion is in tune with stepping out of my comfort zone—and it cuts deep. Deeper than anything else I have felt in life.

- In what ways will stepping out of your comfort zone (by waking up early to work toward a specific goal) be beneficial? How will you feel the passion?

  My answer: At the very least, I will improve my health and fitness by going to the gym, improve my mindset by jumping into the surf afterwards to cool down, improve my connection with my friends by enjoying conversation over a coffee, increase my overall gratitude, and set myself up for a great day.

  After a cold winter swim, I often passionately say to my buddies, "I have never regretted going for an early morning swim." I place a lot of weight on that very small expression of gratitude. Furthermore, I can't remember ever regretting waking up early. If I'm not going to regret it, there's no reason not to do it—and every reason to keep doing it.

I often reflect on how better my life is from stepping out of my comfort zone and can honestly say that it is the best way of improving life—full stop. So set your alarm clock for 5 AM tomorrow, knowing that intentionally stepping out of your comfort zone is your path to success, whatever you choose that to be.

Step 6: Focus on the Positive

The aim of this final step is to celebrate all the wins and benefits you receive from waking at 5 AM. Therefore, you must be creative, even inventive, so that you can overemphasize the positive to induce emotion, excitement, enthusiasm, self-worth, and passion. Whenever doubt or a lack of motivation creeps in, you will then be able to draw on all those advantages of waking at 5 AM to ignite your passion and jump out of bed when that first decision needs to be made. So ask yourself this question: What are your benefits—the advantages—of waking up early? From my experience, I have reflected on the advantages of early rising for many years, and for this section of the book, there are too many to list. Instead, to best help you ignite your passion, I list my top twenty in the following section.

After answering the question to step 6, as you read through the following advantages of waking up at 5 AM, closely reflect on your own life, and highlight those advantages that ring true with you. Not all of them will be directly relevant, but many will be. In any case, wouldn't it be great the next time someone asks you why you wake up so early if you could rattle off a list that ignites not only your passion but maybe theirs too?

TOP TWENTY ADVANTAGES OF WAKING UP AT 5 AM

Over the years of waking up at 5 AM, I feel I have been through it all. I started during a period in my life when I was burnt out, overwhelmed, and lost in an accidental life with no idea how I got there or how to make it better. My strong belief was that by waking up earlier, I could find the time (before the busyness of the day) to work it all out—to live a better life. I didn't even call it a *life of abundance* back then because I hadn't figured out what that even was. I was just waking up early each morning believing that step by step a strategy for tackling each obstacle would unfold, goals would be set, and challenges would be stepped up to.

Now, I can fully appreciate that deciding to wake up at 5 AM each day has exponentially paid off. I am abundant in health and fitness, happiness, family and friends, and wealth—and my desire to shout to the world, "Wake up and live a better life!" is strong.

This book is your guide to fast-tracking my lengthy journey. And this final section in the goal activator chapter on passion is my shout-out to you, so you can make waking up early to live a better life into a passionate kick-start to your day—your magnificent obsession. As you read through the following twenty advantages of waking at 5 AM, connect with those that align with your life and fully commit—play full out—to making them your modus operandi. If you want to make waking up early your passion, it's up to you to activate everything you have read so far in this book and then shout out to the world, "This is my why!"

Enjoy.

1. It's a Positive Start to the Day

There is no better way to kick-start your day than by being successful within the first few seconds. Focus on the positive as the decision alarm goes off, and appreciate that by stepping up now, you have achieved your first goal and taken your first step of the day toward your magnificent obsession. From the very first day you begin waking up at 5 AM, you will be amazed at how naturally that positive action and energy carries over into the rest of your day. Waking up early promotes better development of positive habits that help you reach a higher standard and define who you are and what you're known for doing.

Having a positive start to the day gives you the advantage.

2. It's Time for Yourself

Have you ever considered how much time you actually allocate to yourself? Take a typical day and subtract the time you work, work overtime, run errands, are a parent and partner, clean and maintain the house, buy groceries, pay the bills, volunteer your time—busy, busy, busy. How much time in the day is left over for you? Leaving your goals until the end of the day when you're tired and exhausted is setting yourself up for failure.

One of the greatest benefits of being an early riser is that now you do have the time to work on yourself, and with practice, that becomes a habit and your goals are much more likely to be achieved.

Making the time to work on your own goals first gives you the advantage.

3. It Improves Discipline

How can anyone expect to succeed with challenging and difficult tasks in life when they are unable to get out of bed early and tackle challenges head-on? To achieve a new abundant life, you must exercise discipline. When you master the skill of being disciplined to wake up at 5 AM, as I outline in the first goal activator, you also master the skill of discipline in general, which you can use in all other areas of your life.

Practicing and improving your discipline every morning gives you the advantage.

4. It Enhances Super-Productivity

The hour or two each morning you work on your goals isn't just productive—it's super-productive. Improved productivity naturally results when you work on goals that get you excited and focused. As a 5 AMer, this will be the case because you intentionally choose goals that get you fired up to develop a steadfast plan for achieving them. Beyond that, when you're the first to wake up or first to arrive at work, you receive an enormous advantage: you have a head start on the day. At that time, there are no distractions, no phone calls, no one dropping in for a chat, no children or partners interrupting, and no criticism. It's just you, taking massive action on your goal. I have often found I complete tasks that would otherwise take twice as long or more if done later in the day when distractions or being tired interrupt my workflow.

Uninterrupted time and super-productivity give you the advantage.

5. It Produces More Money and Increases Wealth

Many of the world's most successful people are early risers. And more often than not, successful people earn more money and have a higher level of wealth. After all, I have never heard anyone say, I'm going to sleep in every day to build a business (or any other successful achievement). Being positive, putting yourself first, better discipline, super-productivity, and many more of the advantages listed here will result in great amounts of money and wealth—if that's what you desire.

With improved money and wealth, your standard of living, health, education, comfort, and happiness (up to a level, as I outline in chapter 7) all increase—giving you an advantage.

6. It Increases Your Prospect of Promotion at Work

If your goal is a job or career promotion, then being a 5 AMer is an effective tactic to stand out from the crowd. One way to do that is to always arrive to work early or, even better, be the very first person to arrive at work. As an employer for over twenty years, the team members who arrived to work early always stood out. If they arrived before me, then wow—I was seriously impressed. They still needed to perform over the rest of the day, but being early placed them in clear sight when I was looking for someone to promote. Additionally, arriving early allows for better preparation, super-productivity, being better prepared for meetings, and progressing through projects ahead of schedule—all of which will impress the decision-makers.

Standing out from the crowd gives you the advantage when seeking a promotion.

7. It Improves Studying

By waking early with a well-rested mind and body in an environment free from distractions, you can absorb and retain new information and improve study effectiveness greatly. This is super-productive study time.

During 2006 and 2007, Daniel J. Taylor, assistant professor of psychology at the University of North Texas in Denton, and fellow researchers carried out studies with a sample size of 867 psychology students to examine the relationship between sleep and college academic performance. They concluded, "Students with low conscientiousness are more evening orientated . . . because they do not use time wisely and perhaps procrastinate on schoolwork and projects." Meanwhile, "students on an earlier schedule appear to be more achievement-goal orientated and disciplined."[14] Furthermore, in an article about the study, Taylor goes on to say, "You may be able to increase your grades by making yourself more of a morning person. . . . One way to do that may be to try to get up a half-hour earlier one morning, stick with that schedule for three days or so, and then advance your schedule another 30 minutes." In conclusion, students who regarded themselves as early risers earned better grade point averages than those who regarded themselves as night owls.[15]

Studying is less effective when undertaken at night, usually after a day at work, university, or school. It's obvious why: your brain has been working all day, your body is tired, and stress has taken its toll. Night is not the time to try to learn new things and retain information effectively. Rather, it's the time to unwind and prepare the mind and body for rest, so it can recover and strengthen.

Improved study will give you the advantage.

8. It Optimizes Neuroplasticity

As we learn in chapter 6, through the natural process of neuroplasticity, your brain undertakes physical changes (dependent on the specific environment) that determine the path of thoughts that fire together. The routine of waking early to follow a specific path of thinking places us in an environment that stimulates neuroplasticity. It's quiet, free of distraction, and where focused, repetitive thoughts wire together pathways and networks that become strong habits—hardwired into our way of thinking and taking action.

Waking early encourages neuroplasticity, giving you the advantage.

---

14   Daniel J. Taylor, Karlyn E. Vatthauer, Adam D. Bramoweth, Camilo Ruggero, and Brandy Roane, "The Role of Sleep in Predicting College Academic Performance: Is It a Unique Predictor?," *Behavioral Sleep Medicine* 11, no. 3 (February 2013), https://www.ncbi.nlm.nih.gov/pmc/articles/PMC3959895/.

15   Charlene Laino, "Early Birds Get Better Grades," *CBS News*, June 9, 2008, https://www.cbsnews.com/news/early-birds-get-better-grades-09-06-2008.

9. It Avoids the Morning Rush

You have two options in the morning. Option A: The alarm goes off at the latest possible time to get ready for the day. You quickly shower, rush to get the kids up, hustle to make sure they eat breakfast, push them to dress, and pack lunch. To make matters worse, the dishwasher needs to be packed and turned on, a load of washing hung out to dry, and the house put into some order. Then, you all fly out the door to catch the school bus. Quick, quick, quick, we can't be late! Don't miss the bus! But sometimes you do miss the bus, so it's into the car in a hurry and drive to school in all the congestion, since every other parent seems to be doing the same. Finally arriving at work, you're stressed, on edge, and trying to concentrate (now ineffectively as you're on the back foot). This is madness, but I bet, like me, you can relate!

Option B: Up at 5 AM, and your morning hours are calm, well-organized, and in control. You may have worked on your goals for an hour, but you still have time to get yourself and the children ready for the day. You feel empowered, and the calmness is carried through the whole day. Your stress is reduced, and you're better positioned to take on the pressures of life.

Choosing to avoid the morning rush gives you the advantage.

10. It Helps You Beat the Traffic to Work

The average time it takes to commute to work varies greatly depending on where you live. However, no matter how much time you spend in a car or on crowded public transport, it can always be spent better. Waking early can place your travel time ahead of peak-hour traffic, reducing your commute time significantly. This would have a major effect on your day by reducing the rush and stress each morning and perhaps allowing you to utilize those super-productive hours at work before your colleagues arrive. Look at your current situation and decide if beating the morning traffic is an option. (And maybe you can beat the afternoon traffic as well by finishing early!)

Waking early to beat the traffic may give you the advantage.

11. It Helps You Finish Your Work Earlier

Waking early doesn't mean more work, longer hours, more pressure, or more tasks to manage. It means working smarter, being super-productive, and (when possible) finishing work earlier. No matter what work means to you, starting the day at 5 AM and arriving to work an hour or more before you would have otherwise will bring positive results to your productivity with targets being hit ahead of schedule—so you can finish early. The days of habitually working late every day just to get through your normal work commitments will be over. Now, you can arrive home to spend time with the children, train in your sporting team, work on a goal, and so much more.

Starting earlier and finishing earlier may give you the advantage.

12. It Gives You Better Sleep

Anecdotally, I sleep better at night when I have risen early that morning. During periods when I don't rise early, such as when on a holiday, it's often harder for me to fall asleep. My sleep seems to be lighter, more interrupted, and I feel tired and less energized when I wake up. Without offering medical advice (as I'm basing my guidance on my own experience), when someone remarks that it takes too long to fall asleep or they wake up during the night with difficulty in returning to slumber, then I suggest they start waking at 5 AM. After a few mornings, each night will welcome an earlier bedtime that is more likely deeper and uninterrupted. Sleep deprivation is a serious complaint resulting in slow thinking, a reduced attention span, worsened memory, and lack of energy. For me, I wouldn't be reaching for the sleeping tablets but rather the alarm clock, setting it for 5 AM. After all, there is nothing to lose but much to gain.

Having a better night's sleep is an advantage, for sure.

13. It Makes Every Day a New Opportunity

Nothing gets the blood pumping like doing something new. The passion of new love, the excitement of a new holiday, the smell of a new car, the playfulness of a new puppy, the achievement of a new goal, or the acceptance of a new challenge. You cannot help but feel exhilarated with all this new stuff. However, it's true that nothing stays new forever.

Yet, by waking at 5 AM and building a new mindset, we are practicing a fresh outlook that everything has a new start. After all, every morning is a new day. Every time that sun rolls over the horizon and shines light into our day, it is literally a new start. It's a new opportunity to make this a great day, new words to write in a book, new muscles to exercise at the gym, new healthy foods to eat, new conversations to have over coffee, new laughs to share with our family, new businesses to create, new challenges to tackle, new gratitude for what we have, a new spring to our step, a new view of the world, a new adventure, and a new abundant life to design. Isn't that a better way to see your world?

Every day is a new day—that's your advantage.

14. It Improves Diligence

When someone is diligent, they undertake persistent exertion of the mind or body to accomplish a goal. A diligent person is not overwhelmed by the magnitude of their dream. Instead, they know and practice the skill of taking steady and careful action toward achieving success.

If there are ten steps or a million steps required for the goal to be achieved, the diligent person starts at the beginning and persistently takes action, day after day, until the result is obtained. They are highly motivated and energetic, knowing the journey they are on is one with purpose and direction. They understand there are no shortcuts; yet, at the same time, they take the shortest route. They seek out the answers and readily take on the help of experts to assist in their quest. They stay true to their vision and resist distractions that may take them away from their destination.

Waking every morning to work toward successfully achieving a goal is being proactive in diligence—without a doubt, one of the greatest characteristics to possess—and will always result in success.

Improved diligence is your advantage.

15. It Improves Method

The procedure of taking action in accordance with a definite plan and in a logical and strategic way is known as the *method*. All too often, we embark on a goal or even a life without method. The result is an unplanned and chaotic outcome. We spend months and years working toward goals in an unproductive and inefficient manner, which often results in giving up or perceived failure.

Therefore, the method we take in achieving success is all-important. Method, as I outline in the strategies of this book, when exercised each morning at 5 AM, grows and strengthens. It gains momentum to accelerate your progress toward your goals, and it spins over into the rest of your life.

Without method, life is at worst chaotic and at best inefficient, resulting in regretful lives and lost dreams. With method, life is under control. Method allows us to live fully and without regret. Method converts our goals into reality.

Developing method is your advantage.

16. It Helps You Become More Reliable

In a busy life, it seems unavoidable that we run out of time to do the things we say we will. After all, who can blame us for not allowing enough time to accomplish it all? Doesn't everyone who's busy leave booking a table at their favorite restaurant until the last minute, when it's already booked out? And who isn't always a bit late arriving to catch up with friends? Those small letdowns seem to be acceptable in modern life as careers, workloads, and commitments compete for attention. But as they accumulate over time, a reputation for being unreliable is established.

Yet, if you achieve the opposite by becoming reliable, you will stand out from the crowd and be even more highly appreciated and well-regarded. Waking at 5 AM can give you the time and headspace to better plan your commitments. You can become punctual with those who depend on you. Your family will feel loved and respected with your dedication and increased time for them. Your friends will appreciate that you are trustworthy and live by what you say. Opportunities will flood in as decision-makers are more willing to include you in their dealings. Business acquaintances will see your punctuality and reliability as a foundation for a strong association with you.

You will be someone who walks the walk, instead of talking the talk! Being unreliable repels success. Being reliable attracts it. That's your advantage.

17. It Increases Gratitude, Happiness, and Health

When you rise at 5 AM and start the morning achieving your goals, you will feel happier, healthier, grateful for each new day, and immensely satisfied with your self-worth.

Rising at 5 AM increases happiness in so many ways. Watching the sunrise in the morning is one of the day's most inspirational moments. Enjoying this tranquility with a cup of coffee, appreciating the crisp morning air or chirping birds, quietly reading the newspaper, taking a walk or jog, or simply being alone with your thoughts will increase happiness. And as you become happier and more satisfied with life, you become healthier.

Research has concluded that happier people and those who were more satisfied with their lives reported better health—self-rated health, the absence of limiting or long-term conditions, and physical health. In addition, the results suggested that improving happiness or life satisfaction might also result in better future health.[16]

Endeavoring to pursue your dreams by waking early to productively work on goals not only produces happiness but also fosters better health and stimulates gratitude.

You have everything to be grateful for and that helps you live the best life you can. That's your advantage.

---

16 M. Mohammad, M. Spittal, and G. J. Singh, "Happiness and Life Satisfaction Prospectively Predict Self-Rated Health, Physical Health, and the Presence of Limiting, Long-Term Health Conditions," *American Journal of Health Promotion* 23, no. 1 (2008), https://doi.org/10.4278/ajhp.061023137.

18. It Encourages Self-Improvement

By rising at 5 AM, you can now focus on self-improvement in any area of your life where you feel deficient—exercising, studying, reading, practicing, researching, business and working, using creativity, connecting with yourself—anything is up for improving every morning.

One of the greatest benefits of waking up at 5 AM is that it doesn't compete with any other self-improvement strategy or practice. Rather, it makes these strategies better. Waking early with the clear intent of putting what has been learned into practice greatly advances the results. The risk of failing is reduced simply because you have moved your self-improvement practice to the beginning of the day before it can be overridden or forgotten.

Waking at 5 AM is the time to fast-track self-improvement. That's the advantage that helps you grow and develop into the person you desire to be.

19. It Shows Success at Every Stage

So you woke up at 5 AM, as planned, to work on something very important (a goal or magnificent obsession). That is success, pure and simple.

I have lost count of the number of times I have heard someone of importance, experience, and success say words to the effect of, "Enjoy the journey, not just the end goal."

When it comes to success, we can be too hard on ourselves. Waking up as planned to work on a goal *is* being successful already. Each small step needs to be celebrated with great enthusiasm. After all, we don't have a cheer team following us around, so it's up to us to acknowledge our own success. No one else.

I'm sitting up at our farm, writing this book, having gone for a horse ride this morning before sunrise. If I measure myself against best-selling author John Grisham today, I feel disheartened. However, if I'm more honest with myself and think in line with how I have lived my new abundant life, I am already successful. I'm spending a few days at our farm, feeding the cattle, riding my horse, and being an author. My business continues to run back in Sydney, without my direct attention. I feel healthy, content, and happy.

Tomorrow, I'll head back home to my wife and kids to again swim in the ocean with my surf club buddies and continue to work on living life to its maximum, which is great fun! My life used to be out of control, but I redesigned it. That's the definition of success to me.

I don't say all this to impress you. I say it to impress upon you that no matter what stage of achieving your goals you're at, even if it's the very first day, you can acknowledge that you're already successful. Don't compare yourself to those who are further down the path.

This gives you a huge advantage and helps make waking early a passionate start to the day.

20. It Is the Meaning of Your Life

The meaning of life—it's the all-important question asked and philosophized on throughout history. It sounds like I'm getting very deep about waking up early. Well, I am. Finding passion often requires a completely different perspective.

Therapist, Holocaust survivor, and author Viktor E. Frankl proposes in *Man's Search for Meaning* that the meaning of life is always changing and never ceases: "For the meaning of life differs from man to man, from day to day and hour to hour. What matters, therefore, is not the meaning of life in general, but rather the specific meaning of a person's life at a given moment."[17]

Frankl goes on to explain that there is constant conflict between what we have achieved in life so far and what we want to achieve in the future. "Such tension is inherent in the human being," he writes, "and therefore is indispensable to mental well-being."[18]

Tension, frustration, impatience, pressure, and the fear that you are running out of time are the alarms highlighting the gaps between what you have achieved in life so far and what you want to achieve in the future. Every

17 Viktor Frankl, *Man's Search for Meaning* (Beacon Press, 2006), 131.

18 Frankl, *Man's Search for Meaning*, 127.

strategy and method outlined in this book helps you wake up early to move from your current situation to that of successfully achieving a goal, no matter its size or significance. This means that waking up early can be your meaning in life—closing the gap between where you are and where you want to be.

There is no better reason to wake up early, that's your advantage.

A NEW DAWN BREAKS

I woke up this morning in the silence of the farm and looked at my clock. 4:57 AM. Three minutes before my decision alarm. Outside, the world was pitch dark. For a moment, I listened to the creaking of the house and the easterly wind against the window. In the darkness, I considered rolling over for the three minutes before my phone would gently remind me that it was decision time.

But last night, I had prepared myself. You see, I had spent all day yesterday working with the cattle in the paddocks and had already decided that this morning was dedicated to successfully achieving one goal—finishing the draft of my manuscript. Nothing else mattered. That was my why. As the clock silently ticked, I sensed my heart quicken as the excitement of successfully achieving that goal was building, escalating, and growing.

Before 5 AM, I stepped up.

It was one of those magical mornings when the comfort of bed presents no distraction, and after washing my face with cold water, I made an espresso and then quietly walked outside onto the front lawn.

First light was yet to stretch over the horizon. Squinting my eyes, the silhouettes of fence posts, cattle, and trees were hard to make out, but I could just glimpse a thick blanket of fog sitting peacefully over the lower-lying paddocks. The birds hadn't started their morning calls yet, so the farm was silent. I always like to say good morning to the horses when I'm at the farm. This morning, however, they were out there somewhere in the darkness, enshrouded by fog, and no doubt waiting for the breakfast that would soon be coming.

Slowly drinking my coffee, I could see the sun's first light approaching the horizon. A new day was beginning. *How perfect*, I thought to myself. But I had a goal to achieve, one that was years in the making. So, after breathing in the morning energy from the awakening dawn, I took a final sip, turned, and went back inside to start writing.

Within seconds, I'd fired up my computer. Time to seize the morning.

As I typed, it hit me that the last fifteen years or so have been an amazing journey. Without making that one decision all that time ago to start waking up at 5 AM, my life would now be vastly different.

Had I not challenged myself to wake up early to take control of my future, I might still be living that accidental life—the one that had trapped me and was slowly breaking me.

This is the advantage of simply waking earlier to give yourself the time to take massive action. In fact, that single decision resulted in more beneficial changes to my life than any other decision I have made. I am literally living a new life—a new abundant life—that I designed myself. It might not be perfect, but it's not meant to be.

As you now appreciate, I love to challenge myself. Making the decision to write this book may be one of the hardest yet. I know there are many other authors with much more talent and writers who would have smashed out a book in a fraction of the time. But for me, progress was a hard slog. While I stumbled through the words, structure, and direction, I knew an important message was in there somewhere, but I needed clarity and proof that only time and insight can expose.

After years of writing the notes that morphed into a manuscript draft that was rewritten again and again—distractions, setbacks, and charging bulls—it seemed I would never achieve my goal. I felt people around me doubted my ability. It was just another crazy dream.

Yet I knew something they didn't.

I knew that if I followed my hypothesis, my goal of finally completing the book and living an abundant life would be successfully achieved. Over the years, my strategies were put to the test in my real-world experiment, each new challenge requiring updates to my methods that were again retested and modified. Through the pain of rehabilitation, cold mornings swimming in the ocean rock pool, and sheer determination, my strategies were finally defined and outlined in this manuscript. I now know that if not for that drawn-out, hard-tested, challenging process, this book would not serve you as well.

Over all those years, the 5 AM Advantage guided me to achieve my goals. Discipline, persistence, focus, action, and passion are the all-important goal activators I immersed myself in. Practicing these personal characteristics every day became my modus operandi.

Today was no different. My writing came slowly. But I pushed through the morning and into the afternoon. By the day's end, the goal was achieved, and the draft was successfully completed.

I now know that if I can do this, I can do most things.

And I know that if I can do this, you can do the same—and more.

You can step up to any challenge fully prepared by knowing that each battle will test you, stretch you, and shape you. I was not a 5 AMer, but now I am. I was not in control, but now I am. I was not happy, but now I am. I was not an author, but now I am. I was never a jogger, but now I am. It has taken me more than fifteen years to achieve all these results.

You can achieve similar results—and better!—in a fraction of the time now that you have a strategy.

Up to this moment, your path may have seemed uncertain. Your goals may have seemed to be slipping out of reach. You may have buried your dreams because *your* charging bull knocked you off track. Don't delay any longer. Learn from the past. Act now. Make clear your intention, and find your purpose in life. Declare to the world that you have commenced the journey to fulfill your dreams. Live with true passion, and utilize the full force of that passion in successfully achieving the goals that have been beaten down by distractions, self-sabotage, self-limitation, and stagnation.

Step up to the challenge.

Tonight, prepare your sleep for a great awakening. Tonight, prepare your mind to make a bold decision in the morning. Tonight, fully prepare for the new dawn.

Then, seize the morning.

And awaken to your why.

ACKNOWLEDGMENTS

I am grateful for the many things and many people in my life who made this book possible.

The first ten years living on large rural properties with my father, John Chapman, was a time that greatly set up my life's outlook. Riding horses together, pulling calves, driving around the paddocks in the back of the ute (pickup truck), eating freshly shot rabbit and wild mushrooms, fishing under the shade of a willow tree and watching the platypus swimming below in the crystal-clear water–what an adventure! This was a childhood I was extremely fortunate to experience. During the process of writing my accidental life journal, I read many old letters from Dad's friends and work colleagues sent both before and after his death. That insight into the man I now only distantly remember was a gift I am deeply thankful for. He was a strong man with a reputation as big as the country we live in. Men like that are a rare breed. The few memories of him have been rerun over and over for forty-five years now, and I am grateful to have had such a great dad to help me determine what it means to be a man. I thank him, and I know he would have loved growing old with us.

My mother, Adele Chapman, shared with me her love and passion for the things in life that deeply moved her: a view of a mountain, a song written and played on the piano, her love of the land. She blessed me with passion, and my dreams were always easy to express openly to her—such a wonderful gift. I thank her.

The lives of my sisters, Lorraine and Roz, were equally knocked off track in childhood. Writing this book has allowed me to understand how hard that was—and still is—for them as well. I feel them and will always love them both.

Today, I am grateful beyond measure to have such a loving family, and this book's dedication to my wife, Fiona, and our children, Jess, Ollie, Oscar, and Brooke, cannot be expressed enough. Fiona intimately shared my vision of creating family homes both by the beach and on the farm, so our children always have a stable, safe, and nurturing refuge that equally encourages outdoor action and adventure. She has always supported my beliefs, endured my crazy ideas, and welcomed my passionate outbursts. Her strength, values, and love have helped me become a better man. I am acutely aware that my love for her grows stronger every day. Jess, Ollie, Oscar, and Brooke have always filled my life with happiness, fun, and love. I am so proud of the young adults they have grown to be. I love hanging out with them. They are, without exception, my best friends. I love them all, and I thank them for being my *why*.

I am also grateful to the amazing young ladies who are helping our family grow—Gabriella Wilson and Emily Hayes. My love to them.

I also thank our extended family that reaches from one side of Australia to the other: Chris Walter, James and Charlotte Walter, Georgia Walter and Eric Nguyen, Angus and Madi Chapman, Melany and Sam Marson, Genevieve Chapman, Geoff and Carolyn Deegen, Blake and Rhys Deegen, Karen Galea and Ebony Galea, and Zoe Jo Plunket.

A special tribute goes to Scott Plunket (amazing brother-in-law and favorite beer brewer) and John Chapman (much-loved nephew and incredible brother to Angus, Melany, and Genevieve), who will both be remembered with love for the rest of all our lives.

For the gift of lifelong friendship, I am deeply grateful to Marcel and Lisa Parrett, Tony and Melissa Bellingham, Shayne and Laurence Mulligan, Brad Sewell, Guy (Milo) Vicars, Jo Christie, Sandra Gibney, Annie Phillips, Katie Breatnach, Bronwyn Green, Ted and Sonya Williams, Penny Clements, Philip Rang, Guy Phillips, and Col Green (who I'll forever miss). I thank them.

Special thanks go to my North Narrabeen Surf Lifesaving Club patrol mates, Jason Tydeman, Jamie Paardekooper, Rob McNeil, and Ian Smallman, for listening to me passionately explode in the early morning hours at the gym, rock pool, or beach for over twenty years—poor bastards. The countless miles of swimming in the winter's dark, freezing ocean rock pool have changed my life.

Early manuscript drafts were developed and edited with the help of Katrina Holden, Anita Janik-Jones, Sam Severn, and Mark Williams. I thank them for their enthusiasm for the project by seeing the book's vision and inspiring me to persist with its evolution.

Special thanks go to Ingrid Elfver and Mark Malatesta, who invited me to Colorado to help develop the vision of the early manuscript and help launch my 5 AM coaching.

Thanks also go to my beta coaching clients who greatly supported my mission by volunteering to start waking up at 5 AM: Rodger Glovsky, Jaylynn Venis, Gwenne Gorman, Nicola Baume, Lois Crockett, Siobham Cunningham, Donna DeNomme, and Leah E.

And special thanks go to Paul Allica, champion coaching client, rising actor, moviemaker, and friend for life.

For final publication, a big thank-you goes to Jessica Easto, developmental editor at Greenleaf Book Group. Her pursuit of clarity was challenging—exactly what I needed. Also, I thank the rest of the Greenleaf team: David Endris, Rebecca Logan, Leah Pierre, Jeanette Smith, John van der Woude, Cameron Stein, Scott James, and others who helped me successfully achieve my magnificent obsession of writing this book.

I also thank Tony Robbins, whose passion and inspiration for over thirty years have helped me see that all I needed was within me all along. Additional thanks go to Dean Graziosi, for his dedication in helping authors and coaches find a bigger voice, and Brendon Burchard, whose live seminar in Sydney in 2014 helped set up the direction of my life for the last decade.

Finally, to all my family and friends who have helped me in so many ways on this journey so far:

I'm sorry.

I love you.

Please, forgive me.

Thank you.

ABOUT THE AUTHOR

Photography by Ollie Chapman

BRYCE CHAPMAN'S childhood living on large sheep and cattle stations in Australia was shattered by family tragedy, sending him on a thirty-year trajectory of survival he calls "an accidental life." Burned out from living down to society's standards of success and overwhelmed by the fear of failing to live a better life as he neared forty, he decided on a radical reset. By setting his alarm for 5 AM, he challenged himself to seize each morning and create a new abundant life before the busy demands of the world encroached. Finally, out of the dust of a charging rogue bull came his battle with rehabilitation, persistence, and discipline. He was victorious, and the 5 AM Advantage was born.

Bryce's lengthy experience with waking at 5 AM, along with his unique bush-and-beach lifestyle, gives him a fresh voice that's both direct and supportive, illuminating a path for readers to reach their full potential. Bryce lives harmoniously between a family farm in Lower Hunter Valley and a beachside residence at Narrabeen with his wife, Fiona, and their children.